The Mexican
Revolution

Titles in the World History Series

The Age of Augustus
The Age of Feudalism
The Age of Pericles
The American Frontier
The American Revolution
Ancient Greece
The Ancient Near East
Architecture
Aztec Civilization
The Black Death
The Byzantine Empire
Caesar's Conquest of Gaul
The California Gold Rush
The Chinese Cultural
   Revolution
The Conquest of Mexico
The Crusades
The Cuban Revolution
The Early Middle Ages
Egypt of the Pharaohs
Elizabethan England
The End of the Cold War
The French and Indian War
The French Revolution
The Glorious Revolution
The Great Depression

Greek and Roman Theater
Hitler's Reich
The Hundred Years' War
The Inquisition
The Italian Renaissance
The Late Middle Ages
The Lewis and Clark
   Expedition
The Mexican Revolution
The Mexican War of
   Independence
Modern Japan
The Punic Wars
The Reformation
The Relocation of the
   North American Indian
The Roman Empire
The Roman Republic
The Russian Revolution
The Scientific Revolution
The Spread of Islam
Traditional Africa
Traditional Japan
The Travels of Marco Polo
The Wars of the Roses
Women's Suffrage

The Mexican Revolution

by
**Mary Pierce Frost and
Susan Keegan**

Lucent Books, P.O. Box 289011, San Diego, CA 92198-9011

Library of Congress Cataloging-in-Publication Data

Frost, Mary Pierce, 1961–
     The Mexican Revolution / by Mary Pierce Frost
and Susan E. Keegan.
          p. cm.—(World history series)
     Includes bibliographical references and index.
     Summary: Examines the events leading to, surrounding,
and following the Mexican Revolution.
     ISBN 1-56006-292-4 (alk. paper)
     1. Mexico—History—Revolution, 1910–1920—Juvenile
literature.   2. Mexico—History—20th century—Juvenile
literature.   [1. Mexico—History—Revolution, 1910–1920.]
I. Keegan, Susan E., 1955–   . II. Title.   III. Series.
F1234.F86   1997
972.08—dc20   96-2402
                                                       CIP
                                                        AC

Contents

Foreword

Each year on the first day of school, nearly every history teacher faces the task of explaining why his or her students should study history. One logical answer to this question is that exploring what happened in our past explains how the things we often take for granted—our customs, ideas, and institutions—came to be. As statesman and historian Winston Churchill put it, "Every nation or group of nations has its own tale to tell. Knowledge of the trials and struggles is necessary to all who would comprehend the problems, perils, challenges, and opportunities which confront us today." Thus, a study of history puts modern ideas and institutions in perspective. For example, though the founders of the United States were talented and creative thinkers, they clearly did not invent the concept of democracy. Instead, they adapted some democratic ideas that had originated in ancient Greece and with which the Romans, the British, and others had experimented. An exploration of these cultures, then, reveals their very real connection to us through institutions that continue to shape our daily lives.

Another reason often given for studying history is the idea that lessons exist in the past from which contemporary societies can benefit and learn. This idea, although controversial, has always been an intriguing one for historians. Those that agree that society can benefit from the past often quote philosopher George Santayana's famous statement, "Those who cannot remember the past are condemned to repeat it." Historians who ascribe to Santayana's philosophy believe that, for example, studying the events that led up to the major world wars or other significant historical events would allow society to chart a different and more favorable course in the future.

Just as difficult as convincing students to realize the importance of studying history is the search for useful and interesting supplementary materials that present historical events in a context that can be easily understood. The volumes in Lucent Books' World History Series attempt to present a broad, balanced, and penetrating view of the march of history. Ancient Egypt's important wars and rulers, for example, are presented against the rich and colorful backdrop of Egyptian religious, social, and cultural developments. The series engages the reader by enhancing historical events with these cultural contexts. For example, in *Ancient Greece*, the text covers the role of women in that society. Slavery is discussed in *The Roman Empire*, as well as how slaves earned their freedom. The numerous and varied aspects of everyday life in these and other societies are explored in each volume of the series. Additionally, the series covers the major political, cultural, and philosophical ideas as the torch of civilization is passed from ancient Mesopotamia and Egypt, through Greece, Rome, Medieval Europe, and other world cultures, to the modern day.

The material in the series is formatted in a thorough, precise, and organized manner. Each volume offers the reader a comprehensive and clearly written overview of an important historical event or period. The topic under discussion is placed in a broad historical context. For example, *The Italian Renaissance* begins with a discussion of the High Middle Ages and the loss of central control that allowed certain Italian cities to develop artistically. The book ends by looking forward to the Reformation and interpreting the societal changes that grew out of the Renaissance. Thus, students are not only involved in an historical era, but also enveloped by the events leading up to that era and the events following it.

One important and unique feature in the World History Series is the primary and secondary source quotations that richly supplement each volume. These quotes are useful in a number of ways. First, they allow students access to sources they would not normally be exposed to because of the difficulty and obscurity of the original source. The quotations range from interesting anecdotes to farsighted cultural perspectives and are drawn from historical witnesses both past and present. Second, the quotes demonstrate how and where historians themselves derive their information on the past as they strive to reach a consensus on historical events. Lastly, all of the quotes are footnoted, familiarizing students with the citation process and allowing them to verify quotes and/or look up the original source if the quote piques their interest.

Finally, the books in the World History Series provide a detailed launching point for further research. Each book contains a bibliography specifically geared toward student research. A second, annotated bibliography introduces students to all the sources the author consulted when compiling the book. A chronology of important dates gives students an overview, at a glance, of the topic covered. Where applicable, a glossary of terms is included.

In short, the series is designed not only to acquaint readers with the basics of history, but also to make them aware that their lives are a part of an ongoing human saga. Perhaps they will then come to the same realization as famed historian Arnold Toynbee. In his monumental work, *A Study of History*, he wrote about becoming aware of history flowing through him in a mighty current, and of his own life "welling like a wave in the flow of this vast tide."

Important Dates in the History of the Mexican Revolution

1877	1880–1884	1910	1911	1913	1914	1917	1919	1920

1877
Porfirio Díaz is elected to his first term as president of Mexico.

1880–1884
Gen. Manuel González, a close friend to Díaz, serves one term as president; Díaz returns to office in 1884.

1910
Díaz is reelected to his seventh term as president, but, his government now a corrupt dictatorship, people all over the country begin to revolt; Francisco Indalécio Madero becomes the first popular leader of the revolution by condemning the government, declaring the election a fraud, and calling for Díaz's resignation.

1911
Díaz resigns and escapes to France; Madero is elected president of Mexico, but as he is unable to keep his campaign promises, revolutionary leaders including Emiliano Zapata and Pancho Villa consolidate their power.

1913
Felix Díaz and Gen. Victoriano Huerta lead a coup against the government and have Madero executed; Huerta declares himself president.

1914
Huerta is forced into exile, leaving Mexico without a president; civil war continues to erupt across the country; central leadership is attempted by revolutionary convention; Zapata, Villa, and Venustiano Carranza are among the leaders vying for power.

1917
Delegates to the Constitutional Convention at Querétaro produce the new Constitution of 1917; Carranza is elected president of Mexico.

1919
Zapata is executed by military leaders under the command of Carranza.

| 1923 | 1924 | 1926 | 1928 | 1929 | 1932 | 1934 | 1935 | 1936 | 1938 | 1940 |

1920
At the end of his presidential term, Carranza tries to retain power by choosing his successor, causing a revolt in which Carranza is assassinated while trying to escape into exile; Obregón is elected president; Villa retires as a wealthy ranch owner.

1923
Villa is assassinated while driving to pick up payroll for his employees.

1924
Obregón retires; Plutarco Elías Calles is elected president.

1926
The Cristero Rebellion erupts between supporters of the Catholic Church and the government.

1928
Calles retires; Obregón is reelected president, then assassinated before taking office; Emilio Portes Gil is named provisional president.

1929
Calles organizes National Revolutionary Party (PRN); federal negotiations with the church end the Cristero Rebellion; Pascual Ortiz Rubio is elected president.

1932
Ortiz Rubio resigns; Abelardo Rodríguez is named provisional president.

1934
Rodríguez retires; Lázaro Cárdenas is elected president.

1935
Cárdenas forces Calles into exile.

1936
Cárdenas organizes Confederation of Mexican Workers, allows union leaders into government, and reorganizes the official party as the Party of the Mexican Revolution (PRM).

1938
Cárdenas nationalizes oil and redistributes land.

1940
Cárdenas retires.

After Years of Oppression

There is no way to date the beginning of a revolution. Poverty, desperation, and greed are only a few of the many factors needed to create the frustration and desire for change that bring about violent rebellions. Political and social tensions may simmer beneath the surface of a country's politics for years. However, often it is possible to name the event or catalyst that brings a troubled situation to a crisis point.

In this sense, the Mexican Revolution began when eighty-year-old Porfirio Díaz

The stirrings of revolution began when Porfirio Díaz was reelected as president of Mexico in 1910. His government, the Porfiriato, was an oppressive dictatorship that divided Mexico both racially and economically.

was reelected to his seventh term as president of Mexico in 1910. Díaz's government, nicknamed "the Porfiriato" after the president's first name, was an oppressive dictatorship that divided the country racially and economically. Most Mexicans, because they were poor and uneducated, felt powerless to challenge the government, or even to express their discontent. Though the Constitution of 1857 specifically stated that a president could not serve for longer than four years, by 1910 Díaz had held his office for three decades. Elections were rigged. Candidates for all

public offices had to support Díaz if they wanted to win, because the government manipulated election results to favor its own candidates. Díaz claimed that no one ever ran against him, but in truth his corrupt government silenced potential opponents before they could achieve popular support.

In the elections of 1910, however, Díaz was challenged by a wealthy rancher named Francisco Indalécio Madero. Madero began campaigning against Díaz in 1908, and formed the Anti-Reelectionist

Wealthy rancher Francisco Madero campaigned for president during the 1910 elections. Madero hoped to establish a democratic government and extend freedoms for all Mexicans.

Madero's rebellion against the Porfiriato inspired people across Mexico to rise up against injustice. A panel from a larger mural by artist David Alfaro Siqueiros depicts the revolt led by Emiliano Zapata.

Party, which was specifically targeted at keeping Díaz from a seventh term. Madero sought more than a new government; he wanted a new way of life for the Mexican people. He believed in democracy and wanted to ensure honest, fair elections that would encourage people to vote. He wanted to establish freedom of speech, so that people could disagree with the government without fear of being jailed or even killed.

Proclaiming these ideals, Madero toured the country denouncing Díaz's government. People knew that the Porfiriato was corrupt, and they listened intently. By the spring of 1910, Madero had considerable support, and people all over Mexico began protesting Díaz's bid for reelection.

Díaz grew concerned over Madero's political opposition; on June 5, 1910, he had Madero arrested, then imprisoned in the city of San Luis Potosí. While in prison, Madero drafted a proposal for a new government called the Plan of San Luis Potosí. The document called upon people to rebel against the Porfiriato and accept Madero as their provisional leader until a legitimate presidential election could be held. Since Díaz controlled the press, articles criticizing the government could not be published in Mexico. But Spanish-language newspapers in the United States could and did publish Madero's Plan of San Luis Potosí; soon it was circulating throughout the United States and Mexico. People rallied behind

Madero, repeating the motto of the Anti-Reelectionist Party: "Effective Suffrage. No Reelection."[1]

Elections were held on June 21 while Madero was locked away, and Díaz claimed victory "amid massive charges of fraud by the Anti-Reelectionist party."[2] Once again, Díaz's government announced that the elections were valid because no one had challenged the existing government.

A Struggle for Justice

The people of Mexico were angered by the election results, but they were not surprised. They were so used to fraudulent elections that many never bothered to vote. Díaz routinely awarded state governorships to his loyal allies, who in turn hired friends and relatives as local officials. Historian Alan Knight writes that during Díaz's presidency "local elections became a sham, conducted amidst apathy and indifference" while politicians themselves remained "irremovable [and] unresponsive to local opinion."[3]

But by November 1910 the people were ready to take action against Díaz's blatant corruption. The common people had grown to love Madero and were disgusted at the treatment he had received. They were tired of being excluded from government. Even the wealthy were eager for change, worried that the aged Díaz could no longer govern effectively. Groups of Anti-Reelectionists participated in demonstrations all over Mexico. They even gathered in front of Díaz's private mansion and threw rocks through the windows. Although Díaz sent armed troops into the streets to control the demonstrators, so many people wanted change that the government could no longer silence them. Mexico was like a volcano beginning to erupt. After years of oppression by foreign countries and by their own government, the people of Mexico yearned for justice. Their struggle exploded into a violent, chaotic revolution that lasted thirty years.

1 The Rise and Fall of the Porfiriato

General Porfirio Díaz had not always been unpopular with the people of Mexico. When he first became president in 1877, Díaz seemed a promising, intelligent leader. He took office as a war hero, having been involved in the execution of Maximilian, Mexico's final European emperor. From the start, Díaz vowed to guide Mexico into the twentieth century as an industrialized nation. In fact, he accomplished this goal.

President Porfirio Díaz helped guide Mexico into the twentieth century by industrialization. During his long presidency, Díaz directed the construction of more than fifteen thousand miles of railroads.

1877 to 1900: Díaz Industrializes Mexico

One of the first things Díaz did as president was direct the construction of railroads. According to historian John Mason Hart, "In the eyes of Díaz and his associates, American and Mexican, railroads were the hope of a prosperous future."[4] Only four hundred miles of track existed

A rural railroad station bustles with travelers and vendors. In addition to allowing people to reach remote villages more easily, the railroads enabled Mexico to participate in world trade.

when Díaz took office; by 1910, more than fifteen thousand miles had been laid. Trains chugged across the country, bringing food and supplies to remote villages once accessible only on foot or horseback.

The railroads made possible the development of several industries in Mexico. Before the railroads, mining operations were limited because rock containing valuable minerals had to be brought out of the mountains in baskets tied to the backs of burros. Trains, however, brought laborers and equipment closer to the mines, and transported ore to distant smelting plants. Mining quickly grew into a major industry. Mexico began to supply the world with silver, copper, iron, lead, coal, and even a little gold.

Agricultural crops were produced on a larger scale as well, because the harvest could be transported by rail quickly and sold by the ton. Farmers planted thousands of acres with coffee, sugar, and henequen, a plant used to make rope. In the towns along the rail lines, food processing plants and factories were built for making cloth, paper, and glass. Train cars filled with goods headed to markets all over the country. People rode the trains, too, traveling many miles in search of work.

Most significantly, historian Frederick Katz notes, "The first railway line between Mexico and the United States was inaugurated in 1884," and U.S. companies began investing in Mexico at a "breathtaking pace."[5] Now, for the first time, heavy equipment like tractors and construction machinery could be shipped into Mexico by U.S. firms interested in building factories. North American engineers rode the trains into Mexico to oversee development of huge mining operations and ore-smelting plants. Timber was harvested, too, then shipped by rail back to the United States, where it was milled into lumber and paper. Trains returned to Mexico loaded with finished products such as furniture and automobiles, which sold quickly to prosperous Mexicans.

Díaz's plan had worked; the railroads allowed Mexico to participate in world trade. "For the first time since Maximilian's defeat," writes Katz, "Mexico had diplomatic relations with all major European countries."[6] Industry, funded by foreign investment, expanded all over the country. And because Mexico remained relatively peaceful under Díaz's rule, the population increased from 10 million in 1877 to more than 15 million by 1900.

Hoping to improve their wages and working conditions, thousands of Mexican workers went on strike after the Mexican economy plummeted in the early 1900s.

The standard of living for many Mexicans even increased a little during this time. After 1900, however, the economy took a tumble, and workers became restless.

1900 to 1910: Too Many Foreign Investors

Until 1900, the Porfiriato had been very successful at quieting protest. If a group of coal miners went on strike asking for better working conditions, the military would show up to break up demonstrations, by force if necessary. But after 1900, Mexico began sliding into an economic depression. Living and working conditions for the lower and middle classes grew unbearable. So many people began participating in uprisings against the Porfiriato that the military could no longer stop them. Thousands of workers went on strike, and national opposition movements began calling for the overthrow of the government.

No single problem led to this turn of events. But a central issue was the way the Porfiriato handled foreign investment.

Díaz needed huge amounts of money to modernize Mexico, but his government was often short of funds. Thus foreign investment seemed to offer an ideal way to finance large industrial projects, and Díaz's agents traveled to major cities in the United States and Europe to negotiate deals with wealthy bankers. These foreign investors were eager to control huge money-making operations in Mexico. The Mexican emissaries were equally enthusiastic about the transactions because they skimmed the profits to amass personal fortunes.

For example, Díaz funded construction of his cross-country railroad by selling the railroad contracts to foreign investors. Businessmen from the United States saw an opportunity to make millions importing and exporting goods between the two countries, and indeed, these rich investors grew richer. "By 1902," writes Hart, "a remarkable consortium of U.S. capitalists held 80 percent of Mexico's railroad stock. That sum, over $350 million, constituted about 70 percent of the total U.S. investments in the country."[7] This arrangement was far more beneficial for the United

States than it was for Mexico. Most of the profits from the railroads were siphoned from Mexico to the United States, along with load after load of timber, ore, and sugar. It seemed the Porfiriato was giving away Mexico's most valuable resources.

Oil was another resource costly both to pump from the ground and to process, so Díaz sold drilling rights to foreigners. One of the most persistent oilmen to drill wells in Mexico was Weetman Pearson of Great Britain. When Pearson discovered oil near Tampico on the Gulf coast of Mexico, the Porfiriato sold him the land, practically giving away some of the richest oil fields in the world. Pearson made a fortune exporting Mexican oil to Europe. He even sold some of it back to Mexico. Eventually, Pearson controlled the single largest economic enterprise in the country.

The great mines of Mexico were also turned over to foreigners, who had the capital and engineering experience needed to build ore-extracting works around the rich veins of silver, copper, and other minerals. According to Hart:

> Of the thirty-one major mining companies operating in Mexico during the last years of the Porfiriato, United States capitalists owned seventeen and held 81 percent of the industry's total capital. Their British counterparts held ten of the companies and 14.5 percent of the total capital. Mexican owners operated only a few concerns.[8]

The Porfiriato was happy with this system because the foreign companies greatly expanded mining operations in Mexico, and paid the government a percentage of their profits. Also, the companies provided thousands of jobs for local labor. Foreign investors were happy, too, because the mines were so productive, and because Mexican laborers would chip out the rich ores for a few cents a day.

The drawbacks, then, were experienced by the laborers. Desperate to earn money to buy food, they worked hard with no hope of receiving pay raises or promotions. The best jobs were usually held by foreigners, or the relatives of government officials. Profits from the mines went to the Mexican government, or left the country along with the boxcars of raw ore.

Unemployment, Homelessness, Starvation

Between 1900 and 1910, European and American companies bought more than $3 billion worth of Mexican land, minerals rights, agricultural enterprises, and factories. At first, these investments seemed to help Mexico maintain economic stability. But when demand for raw materials dropped in the North, Mexico reacted like a puppet released from its strings. In 1907 and 1908, the United States faced its own economic recession, and a number of investors could no longer afford to stay in Mexico. They walked away from their businesses, taking whatever money was left. Textile plants and mines suddenly had no owners, no managers, and no money for payroll. Thousands of laborers lost their jobs.

To make matters worse, millions of peasants were homeless. By 1894, Díaz had sold about one-fifth of the entire country, more than 134 million acres of public lands, to foreign investors or cronies. Much of this land had belonged to native Indian communities for centuries.

Many peasants were left impoverished and homeless when the government let foreign investors purchase land that had belonged to native Indian communities.

Historian Lesley Byrd Simpson describes the situation:

> When the Indians objected, as did the Maya and the Yaqui, the army and the Rurales (government police) put down the "rebellions," and thousands of prisoners were sold into slave gangs. . . . By the end of the Díaz regime not ten per cent of the Indian communities had any land whatever.[9]

This chain of events left the poorest segment of society unable to grow food to feed their families. Small, family-run farms that remained were further affected by drought, poor water irrigation, infestations of locusts, and unchecked plant diseases. Between 1907 and 1910, crops failed and famine began claiming lives throughout central and northern Mexico. The government imported inexpensive, low-grade corn to feed the starving peasants, but not enough to keep people from dying. At the same time, foreign companies that owned vast, modern, well-irrigated agricultural projects continued to export coffee, sugar, and vegetables. Once again, Mexicans had to stand aside as their finest products left the country.

Peasant women suffered the most during this time, because the national constitution adopted by the government in 1857 failed to mention them at all. Women had no legal rights, nor any chance of getting an education or a decent job. Unable to read or write, many unmarried women turned to prostitution to survive. In 1908, Luis Lara y Prado, a physician and social critic, noted that "12 percent of all the women in Mexico City between the ages of fifteen and thirty were listed as prostitutes."[10]

A peasant woman makes tortillas in her makeshift kitchen. Without legal rights, education, or decent jobs, peasant women continuously struggled to provide for themselves and their families.

Landless Peasants

Donald Hodges and Ross Gandy describe the life of an average peasant worker in the early 1900s in Mexico 1910–1982: Reform or Revolution?

"On the semi-feudal haciendas in central Mexico the peon sweated from dawn to dark, forever in debt to the company store [where most workers were required to buy their food]. He slept on a straw mat in a filthy hut with two rooms for his family. When he fathered a child he knew it would probably die: the infant mortality rate was higher than in Asia. The water was bad, and horrible diseases crept about. The peon's diet was the eternal tortilla and the bean, and he was lucky to have it: in Mexico thousands starved to death every year. If he ran away the mounted police hunted him down and dragged him back. If he stole a peso he had to face the lashes of the foreman. . . . Sometimes the poor revolted against their masters, but these revolts were quickly crushed."

Life for many Mexican peasants was bleak, consisting of hard physical labor and poor living conditions.

On the plantations, single women working as laborers were frequently forced to marry complete strangers, because ranch owners would "give" women to the field bosses as a way of granting favors. The women had no say in the matter. Once married, a woman could not collect the wages she earned because her husband was legally entitled to all her money. As Shirlene Ann Soto notes in her study of women of the Mexican Revolution, these women were virtually enslaved: "Once married, a woman committed herself for life. Divorce was unknown in the 1880s—and unthinkable."[11] Indian women, dragged from their homes by soldiers or wealthy landowners, were forced to work in factories or fields as slaves. To make matters worse, they were often raped, first by the soldiers transporting them, then again by plantation owners and field bosses.

Though slavery was illegal, it was unofficially practiced during the Porfiriato. The military plundered Indian villages to "collect" both women and men to work for the railroads, factories, and plantations. Instead of receiving money for their efforts, these laborers were given credit at company-owned stores, where they were forced to buy food and clothing at inflated prices. Frederick Katz writes that these laborers "were not allowed to leave their estates until their debts had been repaid," and ranch owners made sure "by fraud [and] by overcharging in the company store . . . that these debts could not be repaid."[12] Conditions could not have been more degrading or oppressive.

Científicos: The Scientists of Racism

How could the Porfiriato stand aside while such atrocities were being committed against the Mexican people? Many government officials, including Díaz, held racist beliefs. In the early 1900s, a philosophy called positivism became popular among the elite classes of Europe and Mexico.

Positivists, called *científicos*, or "scientists," in Mexico, actually believed that Mexicans of European origin were wealthy and educated because they were more highly evolved than the peasant classes. The so-called *científicos* declared that poor, uneducated Indians were the least evolved members of the human race, capable only of hard, physical labor. Mestizos, people of both Spanish and Indian ancestry, fell somewhere in the middle of this most unscientific of evolutionary scales. Those with European blood and whiter skin were said to be the most evolved.

Científicos advanced these racist ideas to justify programs that protected their own comfortable positions in society. Not all wealthy, educated Mexicans accepted positivism. But Díaz's closest advisers were *científicos*, and the president listened to them. All over Mexico, people in positions of power took advantage of peasant labor, and Díaz did nothing to stop it.

Native Mexicans, who knew they were being exploited, despised the Porfiriato. They had little choice in the matter, however. If they appealed to local officials for protection and fair labor practices, they were ignored. If they fought for their rights, they were killed, imprisoned, or sent to slave camps. This is why the peasant population was so eager to participate in the revolution. When Francisco Madero asked these people to join him in overthrowing the government, they were quick to respond.

Champagne in the Face of Starvation

In the fall of 1910, Porfirio Díaz seemed oblivious to the problems facing his people. The Porfiriato was proud of itself for industrializing the country, and its wealthy

President Díaz (fourth from left) and many of his advisers believed in positivism—a racist philosophy that proclaimed Mexicans of European descent were more highly evolved than the peasant classes.

members celebrated Díaz's "reelection" in Mexico City. One hundred sea turtles, prized for their meat, were brought in from the coast. Crates of fresh river trout and a boxcar full of champagne arrived for several lavish banquets. Books describing the Porfiriato's achievements, published just for the occasion, were given as party favors. One asked its readers, "Have we not conquered the difficulties of more than three-quarters of a century passed in civil and international wars . . . ? This in itself guarantees that . . . we shall conquer all other inconveniences placed in our way."[13]

But as Díaz's aging generals bragged about Mexico's economic stability and success, millions of outraged people across the nation prepared to overthrow the government. Members of the wealthy upper class wanted to gain control of Mexico's resources to prevent the continued flow of profits out of the country. The middle class wanted better jobs, more and better schools, access to health care, and a chance to participate in what had become a dictatorial government. Peasants were sick of being used as slaves and treated as inferior members of society. Indians wanted the land of their ancestors returned so that they could raise their own food and live independently, with dignity. Everyone wanted the chance to live a decent life.

The corrupt Porfiriato ignored Mexico's starving peasants while it generously financed extravagant banquets for foreign

Throughout Mexico citizens armed themselves and prepared to overthrow the corrupt Porfiriato, hoping to achieve a better way of life through their struggles.

ambassadors, an insult too flagrant for the masses to ignore. The people of Mexico refused to accept Díaz as their president for another term. They gathered whatever weapons they could find and prepared to fight.

Chapter

2 Leaders of the Revolution

The Mexican Revolution had no single leader and no single agenda. The middle and upper classes wanted one kind of reform for the country, while peasants wanted another. For this reason, various revolutionary leaders emerged with distinctly different goals and methods. The most well known, like Francisco Indalécio Madero, Pascual Orozco, Pancho Villa, and Emiliano Zapata, had enormous followings. Others led perhaps a few hundred peasants and are little noted by historians. One thing all of these revolutionaries had in common, however, was a desire to remove Díaz from the presidency.

Madero: Optimism and Persistence

The man who would effectively challenge the Díaz government, Francisco Indalécio Madero, was born October 30, 1873, the oldest son of one of the richest, most established families in northern Mexico. His grandfather Evaristo Madero, who served under President Díaz as governor of the state of Coahuila between 1880 and 1884, amassed a fortune by investing in cotton plantations, factories, wineries, and mines. While peasants lost their land and jobs un-

Francisco Madero worked to reestablish democracy in Mexico by restoring fair elections and by guaranteeing the constitutional rights of all citizens.

der Díaz's rule, the Madero family prospered and young Francisco was educated at some of the finest schools in the United States and France.

When he returned to Mexico as a young man, Madero began overseeing the

Zapata Explains Morality

Historian John Womack Jr. recalls how Zapata and Madero first met in 1911 in Mexico City in Zapata and the Mexican Revolution.

"Zapata stood up and, carrying his carbine, walked over to where Madero sat. He pointed at the gold watch chain Madero sported on his vest. 'Look, Señor Madero,' he said, 'if I take advantage of the fact that I'm armed and take away your watch and keep it, and after a while we meet, both of us armed the same, would you have a right to demand that I give it back?' Certainly, Madero told him; he would even ask for an indemnity. 'Well,' Zapata concluded, 'that's exactly what has happened to us in Morelos, where a few planters have taken over by force the villages' lands. My soldiers—the armed farmers and all the people in the villages—demand that I tell you, with full respect, that they want the restitution of their lands to be got underway right now.'"

family's cotton plantations and the peasant labor force that worked them. Biographer Stanley R. Ross writes that Madero was a fatherly boss: "He provided his workers with well-ventilated and hygienic living quarters. His personal physician was required to visit the haciendas to care for the sick. With his own funds Madero sustained elementary schools on the properties and required the workers to send their children."[14] Gradually, he became widely respected as a generous and fair businessman.

Madero first became interested in politics in 1903, when the military used gunfire to break up a peaceful gathering in support of a new candidate for state governor. The government had finally gone too far, in Madero's eyes. In order to restore democracy in Mexico, he would have to get involved. So in 1905 he formed the Benito Juárez Democratic Club to support people who ran for office against members of the Porfiriato. It also sponsored two weekly newspapers that discussed people's rights and encouraged them to vote. Government officials were offended by the papers and repeatedly tried to arrest the editors, but ultimately both managed to escape, with Madero's help, in the back of horse-drawn straw carts.

For the next few years, Madero actively encouraged peaceful opposition to the government. Because his family had prospered during the Porfiriato, Madero respected President Díaz, and wanted only moderate change. He saw no need for a revolution, just some political housecleaning. Madero advocated fair elections, the chance to participate in the political process, and guaranteed constitutional rights. But, as he was to discover, he had gravely underestimated the level of government corruption.

In 1908, Porfirio Díaz made a political blunder that opened the door for Madero's political ambitions. While traveling in the United States, Díaz granted an interview to an American journalist named James Creelman in which Díaz stated that he planned to retire in a few years, and that he welcomed opposition to his government. "I firmly believe that the principles of democracy have grown and will flourish in Mexico," Díaz said. "I will forget myself in order to inaugurate with complete suc-

Porfirio Díaz denied any intention of retiring from the presidency and allowing the government to be restructured.

cess a democratic government in the Republic."[15] Creelman's article was translated and reprinted in several Mexican newspapers, and suddenly, all over Mexico political groups formed official parties to oppose the Porfiriato. The Democratic Party was formally launched in Mexico City, and it was at this time that Madero formed the Anti-Reelectionist Party.

Madero Campaigns for President

When Díaz returned to Mexico, he denied his statements to Creelman and announced his intention to run for president after all. Madero decided to run against him. With his wife, Sara, Madero traveled by train all over Mexico, speaking to hundreds of people about their constitutional rights. As part of his campaign, he handed out copies of his book, *La Sucesión Presidencial en 1910*, or *The Presidential Succession in 1910*. Though the book was written for educated businesspeople like himself, his speeches appealed to members of every social class.

The Porfiriato began to worry about Madero's popularity, and shut down his latest newspaper, *El Anti-Reeleccionista*. The Anti-Reelectionist Party, which had replaced the more moderate Benito Juárez Club, also came under attack. Anti-Reelectionist Party meetings were forbidden in some states, as were rallies favoring Madero. Yet thousands continued to support the liberal-minded leader. According to Alan Knight, "10,000 welcomed Madero to Guadalajara, 25,000 to Puebla,"[16] amidst enthusiastic cheering. Madero knew he could win a fair election: Then the aging dictator would have to accept retirement peacefully, and the government could be restructured without violence.

Knight notes that as late as 1909, Madero still "strongly opposed any idea of armed revolution."[17] But on June 16, 1910, just before the elections, Díaz had Madero thrown into prison. The next day, the Porfiriato reported that Madero received a total of just 221 votes, with no votes at all from his hometown. Díaz confidently declared himself president of Mexico for a seventh term, to the public's dismay. Madero petitioned the Mexican Congress, claiming the elections had been fraudulent. Then in early October, Díaz announced that the petition was invalid and again declared himself president.

Determining that Díaz would never pay attention to peaceful demonstrations, Madero decided that gunfire was the only way to force the president from office. However, before Madero could lead a revolution, he had to get out of prison. On October 5, 1910, Madero disguised himself as a railroad mechanic and escaped from San Luis Potosí on a northbound train. Two days later, he crossed the U.S. border into San Antonio, Texas. There, he drafted a hundred-page argument in favor of revolution.

The Plan of San Luis Potosí

Named after the town where Madero had been imprisoned, the Plan of San Luis Potosí was a passionate plea urging people to fight against the government. Groups of people, he wrote, "in their constant effort to obtain liberty and justice, find themselves forced in certain historic moments to make the greatest sacrifices." Mexicans, he explained, faced such a moment because "tyranny oppresses us in such manner that it has become intolerable."[18]

Madero also wrote that the results of the recent elections were meaningless because the government prevented people from voting freely. Until honest elections could be held, Madero would serve as the country's provisional president. He designated Sunday, November 20, 1910, as the first day of the revolution, and expected supporters of his Anti-Reelectionist campaign to challenge government officials all over the country. Since Díaz's military was largely comprised of peasants drafted against their will, Madero invited soldiers to switch sides and fight against Díaz. He expected the revolution to be brief, perhaps a few months; then Madero would begin to restore democracy to Mexico.

But in mid-November, government agents discovered a stash of weapons that had been smuggled into Mexico City by revolutionaries working for Madero. On November 17, the national newspaper announced that a plot against the government had been foiled. Hundreds of people were arrested, including some of Madero's key leaders. What was supposed to be the first official day of revolution, November 20, was marked by a few relatively small uprisings.

Díaz's government thought the revolution was over before it had started. Lord Cowdray, an English oil lobbyist reported, "This affair will be forgotten within a month."[19]

But the government was wrong. Madero's call for revolution had struck a raw nerve in Mexico, and people took up arms against the government all over the country. One historian writes:

Pascual Orozco, a shopkeeper turned revolutionary, fought on behalf of the Mexican people. Orozco was one of the most successful rebel leaders during the early part of the revolution.

The Díaz government was busy stamping out the sparks, but the fires were spreading, disorganized and undirected but effective. Peasants, ranchers, schoolteachers, lawyers, students, and merchants were oiling their rifles, strapping cartridge belts across their chests and stealing off to join self-constituted *jefes* [bosses] of the revolution.[20]

Pascual Orozco, Pancho Villa, Emiliano Zapata

One of the most successful *jefes* of the early revolution was a tall, thin shopkeeper named Pascual Orozco. He had learned how to fight by protecting the metal mines of Chihuahua from armed bandits; after Madero's call to arms he turned these skills against the Porfiriato. By early December 1910, Orozco had successfully captured the important railroad town of Guerrero, the first important victory of the revolution. But Orozco made it clear: He was not fighting on behalf of Madero; he was fighting for the people of Mexico.

About a hundred miles from Orozco's uprising, another man was leading a revolution of his own. He was a stout young cattle rustler named Doroteo Arano, better remembered by his nickname: Pancho Villa. Historian Alan Knight notes that Villa "readily effected the conversion from sierra drifter and bandit to revolutionary *guerrillero*,"[21] or guerrilla leader. Soon he led an army of three hundred men on raids against the villages around San Andrés, near the capital of Chihuahua. Notorious for his storytelling, his arrogance, and his practice of stealing supplies for his men, Villa quickly became a popular revolutionary leader. His followers were known as Villistas.

From the rich, sugarcane-growing state of Morelos, south of Mexico City, emerged another revolutionary leader who did not support the ideals of Madero. Emiliano Zapata, the elected chief of a small village called Anencuilco, was a small but tireless man. Only thirty-one years old in 1911, he was considered a man of some means because his family owned a few horses and lived in an adobe and stone house rather than a hut. Zapata represented peasants who had farmed the mountainous countryside of Morelos for thousands of years. Their land had been confiscated and sold to wealthy hacendados, owners of the

(Above) Guerrilla leader Pancho Villa led an army of three hundred men in his home state of Chihuahua. Meanwhile, Emiliano Zapata (below) organized peasants in Morelos in a revolt against the wealthy landowners.

large estates called haciendas, during the Porfiriato, and Zapata was to lead the fight to gain it back.

Zapata's followers, known as Zapatistas, believed above all else that the peasant classes must be represented in the government before Mexico could call itself a democracy. The Zapatistas were often so poor they carried their few possessions on their backs when they came down from the mountains to attack military garrisons. Barefoot volunteers, the Zapatistas were fierce fighters. They believed in their right to reclaim the land, and they were extraordinarily loyal to their leader. Indeed, Zapata is still regarded as one of Mexico's most sincere, and beloved, leaders.

Hundreds of other revolutionary leaders led localized uprisings for various causes. Each limited revolt contributed to the downfall of the Porfiriato. People fought with any available weapon: guns, bows and arrows, machetes, even rocks. Women fought alongside men and on their own. Dolores Jiménez y Muro, for example, was the president of a feminist organization that protested the Porfiriato's refusal to grant women basic rights. On September 11, 1910, she had organized a demonstration in Mexico City, calling on Mexican women to recognize that their "rights and obligations go much farther than just the home."[22] This demonstration was nonviolent, but Jiménez y Muro was jailed anyway. It was the typical reaction of a government that did not want to acknowledge the depth of unrest felt by the populace.

Disorganized Beginnings

"The beginnings of the revolution were ludicrous,"[23] claims historian Henry Bamford Parkes. The revolutionaries were hopelessly disorganized, united only by abstract ideals and goals, and leaderless. When Francisco Madero crossed the border from Texas into Coahuila, he expected to meet a large armed force, but instead he got lost, and found only twenty-five armed men waiting to join him. Retreating in despair, he was about to give up and sail for Europe when word reached him that Orozco had risen against federal forces in Chihuahua, and, with Pancho Villa, controlled the southern half of the state. Meanwhile, Zapata was recruiting soldiers in Morelos, and had begun attacking wealthy haciendas. Parkes writes that by April 1911 "*guerrilleros* were attacking the *jefes políticos* and the Díaz bureaucracy in Sonora and Sinaloa, Durango and Puebla and Guerrero, Vera Cruz, Tabasco, Oaxaca, and Yucatán. The whole country was beginning to take fire."[24]

Díaz, despite his dictatorial reputation, had done little to stem the tide of revolt. He had been waiting for José Limantour, his minister of finance and right-hand man, to return from New York and straighten everything out. Limantour

Women as well as men participated in uprisings during the Mexican Revolution. These female revolutionaries demonstrate their marksmanship.

José Limantour, Mexico's minister of finance and Díaz's right-hand man, was unsuccessful in negotiating with the revolutionists.

Morelos. People were fighting the government all over Mexico. According to Stanley Ross, "Only five of the thirty-one [states] were untouched by the revolution, and in most of the others the insurgents dominated the major portions."[26]

Pressure continued to mount for Díaz's resignation. At this point the elderly president was ill and bedridden, in constant pain from an abscessed tooth. He finally agreed to step down, in a treaty signed "outside Ciudad Juárez, at 10:30 p.m. on May 21, [1911], over a table illuminated by the arc-lights of automobiles."[27] A non-*científico* Catholic lawyer named Francisco León de la Barra became the provisional president of Mexico; he would rule the country until elections could be held. The next day, Díaz slipped out of the country via Veracruz. He died in exile in Paris on July 2, 1915.

The Provisional Government

With Díaz gone, Madero entered Mexico City and was welcomed by enthusiastic crowds. But his popularity soon began to fade; because he was not yet officially in power, he could not control the activities of the federal government. During the five months and ten days that de la Barra was president, Madero was forced to stand aside helplessly while the government continued its oppressive policies.

Madero's biggest problem was trying to convince de la Barra not to send the federal army out after revolutionary troops. While Madero negotiated in good faith with revolutionary leaders like Zapata, his efforts were undermined by de la Barra's actions. President de la Barra, a

returned on March 19, picked up the reins of government, and promised to make reforms. In April, Díaz backed Limantour's promises, suggesting to Congress "the prohibition of reelection, division of large rural properties, judicial reform, and local autonomy as government policy."[25] Then, Limantour began negotiating with the revolutionaries on behalf of the Porfiriato.

Early efforts at negotiation failed; Díaz refused to resign and the rebels would accept no less. On May 10, Orozco and Villa led their troops to victory, taking Ciudad Juárez from federal forces. Two days later, Zapata's army took the town of Cuautla in

Madero's Triumphal Entry

In Diplomatic Days, Edith O'Shaughnessy recalls the excitement Madero caused when he entered Mexico City shortly after his election. O'Shaughnessy, the wife of an American diplomat, lived in the capital during the early days of the revolution.

"People came from far and near, in all sorts of conveyances or on foot, just to see him, to hear his voice, even to touch his garments for help and healing. . . .

Well, it is a curious experience to see a people at the moment of what they are convinced is their salvation, to see the man they hail as 'Messiah' enter their Jerusalem. I can think of no lesser simile. The only thing they didn't shout was 'Hosanna.' The roofs were black with people along his route. Many threw flowers and green branches as he passed. As for the equestrian statue of [former king of Spain] Charles IV, in the Plaza, it was alive with people, who clung all over it, climbing to the top, sitting on Charles's head, hanging to his horse's tail."

Following the resignation of President Porfirio Díaz, Francisco León de la Barra (pictured) was named provisional president of Mexico. During his five months in office, de la Barra continued the oppressive policies of the Porfiriato.

conservative Porfiriato at heart, ordered federal troops to attack the Zapatistas even as Madero was meeting with them. Historian Stanley Ross writes, "Madero was at a loss—then and later—to explain this brazen subversion of his efforts."[28]

Zapata either did not understand or could not excuse Madero's inability to control the government he proposed to lead. Not sympathetic to Madero's inexperience, Zapata held him responsible for every hostile act taken by de la Barra. This was the conflict that poisoned the relationship between Madero and Zapata even before elections could be held.

Yet Madero remained popular enough to win the presidency. He had come "to symbolize the deep desire for a change—a social and economic, as well as a political, change."[29] So, when elections were held on October 1 and 15, he won by an overwhelming majority. He would

Zapata Wreaks Havoc on the Countryside

American diplomats felt that Emiliano Zapata and his rebels were a dangerous and unruly bunch, as related in this official report from Documents on the Mexican Revolution, *edited by Gene Z. Hanrahan.*

"[D]isorders in a large part of the country continue. The famous bandit Zapata, commanding a force sometimes small in numbers and at other times amounting to two and three thousand men, is overrunning and terrorizing portions of the states of Veracruz, Puebla, Morelos, Guerrero, and Mexico and formidable bands have devastated, burned and destroyed property, and committed all sorts of crimes within forty miles of the gates of the Capital city. The Federal army, which has been sent in constantly increasing force against this bandit, seems either to be incapable of dealing with the situation or, as is freely intimated by the press and in Congress, is restrained by the influence of Madero who is secretly encouraging Zapata for the purpose of overawing the anti-Madero element in the City of Mexico."

Armed and ready, Zapatistas watch for approaching federal troops from their hillside vantage point.

not, however, take office as a revolutionary leader at the height of his power. He entered office with diminished prestige, a cabinet full of conservatives who were ready to attack his plans, and constituency still desperate for change. Madero thought the revolution was almost over; in fact, it had barely begun.

Chapter

3 Failed Campaign Promises

Madero was sworn into office on November 6, 1911, but his government was already in trouble. The revolutionaries who had conspired to rid the country of Porfirio Díaz had never discussed their various needs and goals. As it turned out, they all wanted different things.

Madero's goal was to convert a dictatorial government into a democracy. According to one historian, the new

Newly elected president Francisco Madero (seated) and his cabinet. Although Madero had great expectations for his administration, his endeavor was doomed from the start.

Finally, a Free Election

In this letter to a U.S. senator, reprinted in Blood Below the Border, *an American consul living in Mexico describes a recent election in Mexico. President Madero insisted that the election be free, even though political representatives might be elected who disagreed with his policies.*

"A federal election had just been held, and, for the first time in the history of Mexico, every [adult male] citizen had the privilege of casting his ballot. Heretofore the ballot was cast by a few politicians for the whole voting population. It was very noticeable that the middle and lower classes took a serious view of their responsibilities, and the election passed off very orderly.

The higher classes, in many instances, held aloof from voting with the lower classes and, with the usual Mexican [lack of] foresight, did not realize until it was too late that they had handed the reins of government over to the middle and lower classes, with the result that strong arm rulers with long experience in governing the Mexican people were replaced with inexperienced rulers, who were honest enough in their purpose to lift the lower classes, yet lacked the experience and especially the decision and firmness necessary to hold down the class of Mexicans that take 'liberty' for license to plunder and kill."

president "believed in democratic principles, had confidence in the ability of people to govern themselves, and hated the bossism and militarism which had characterized Mexican government for most of its one hundred years of uneasy independence."[30] Madero thought that free elections and freedom of expression would be enough to improve the health of the nation.

But Emiliano Zapata and his Morelos rebels envisioned a much more radical economic and political revolution. They wanted the new government to return the ancestral lands that the Porfiriato had sold off to foreign corporations. In the northern states, the large armies headed by Pancho Villa and Pascual Orozco also fought for land reform.

Meanwhile, Díaz's followers, the conservative *científicos*, still controlled industry and banking. They opposed the revolution and everything it stood for. Those who had supported Madero during the elections of 1911 did so because they saw him as one of their own, someone they trusted to make as few changes as possible. The *científicos* were prepared to fight to maintain their power and privileges. The military, too, preferred the political structure developed by Díaz, and joined the *científicos* in their antirevolutionary stance.

Zapata's Plan de Ayala

Thus Francisco Madero, a political novice and liberal idealist, was elected to rule a fractured society. Madero's position on agrarian reform was not aggressive enough for Emiliano Zapata and his followers, who wanted to reclaim their ancestral lands from the government immediately. Only two weeks after Madero took office, on November 25, 1911, Zapata issued the Plan de Ayala, which formally demanded the return of ancestral lands and declared that the revolution was turning against Madero.

This challenge would prove to be insurmountable.

Zapata's plan was based on restoring agreements that had been broken under the Díaz regime. During the years of Díaz's rule, ancient *ejidos*, or land collectives, which had fed entire villages for centuries, were stolen by government surveyors working on behalf of wealthy hacendados. Peasants who lost their lands faced severe hunger and poverty; they initiated uprisings across the country, and some even submitted plans for agrarian reform to the Porfiriato. But protest was always repressed by the military, or simply

Emiliano Zapata (seated, center) and his followers issued the Plan de Ayala on November 25, 1911, demanding national agrarian reform and declaring that the revolution was turning against Madero.

ignored. Zapata's Plan de Ayala included principles expressed in previous plans, but was far more radical because it denounced Madero's government and insisted that failure to return lands would result in a nationwide civil war.

When Zapata met with government officials to defend the plan, he declared:

> I've been Señor Madero's most faithful partisan. I've given infinite proofs of it. But I'm not any more. Madero has betrayed me as well as my army, the people of Morelos, and the whole nation. Most of his [original] supporters are in jail or persecuted, and nobody trusts him any longer because he's violated all his promises. He's the most fickle, vacillating man I've ever known.[31]

The Plan de Ayala also labeled Madero "a traitor to the fatherland" and called for the northern revolutionary Pascual Orozco to become the new head of state. But the plan's central provision and most enduring legacy was national agrarian reform. Large portions of land would be taken from the richest landowners and redistributed to peasants. Anyone who opposed the plan would automatically lose their land to the government on the grounds that they were traitors to the nation.

Zapatistas Fight for Their Land

Madero sympathized with the plight of landless peasants, but he thought the Plan de Ayala was too demanding and too radical. So he ignored it, making a naive political blunder. Late in November 1911, Zapata led the state of Morelos into open rebellion. Throughout 1912, Zapata's troops attacked haciendas and federal installations, disrupted communications,

Madero: Mountebank or Messiah?

U.S. ambassador Henry Lane Wilson's memoir, Diplomatic Episodes in Mexico, Belgium, and Chile, *shows that he grew to scorn Francisco Madero.*

"The revolution of Madero sprang unarmed and motley from the national discontent with the system and administration of the Díaz régime. This discontent it neither represented nor organized. Madero was a comparatively unknown person who appeared at a psychological moment and reaped a harvest which might have gone to stronger and abler men had any such been then prominent in the public eye. His previous history had been that of a dreamer of dreams, but he was more of a mountebank than an messiah; an honest enthusiast with a disorganized brain."

and destroyed transportation systems. The Zapatistas took, then lost, town after town as Madero's government sent federal troops to suppress the revolutionaries. The government even declared martial law, which meant that the military could overrule the constitutional rights of the people. Still, the Zapatista revolt continued to escalate as peasants became increasingly desperate to reclaim their land. Fighting spread quickly to states south and east of Morelos, including Puebla, Guerrero, Tlaxcala, and Mexico.

What Madero failed to realize was that Zapatismo, as the philosophy of Zapata's followers was called, was more than a personality cult drawn to Emiliano Zapata. It was an emotional movement based on historical and cultural values. Participants wanted Mexico to return to the days in which land was communally owned, when village chiefs decided the fate of the villagers, and when community ruled a person's life. Madero assumed the Zapatista movement was a political movement, but it was more. This revolution was about people's desire to control their own resources and to overcome barriers of ethnicity and economic status. Zapata was not calling for peace, progress, democracy, or any other abstract ideals because he was not an ideologue. On the contrary, "the movement had suffered from its leader's excessive fondness for 'good horses, fighting cocks, flashy women, card games and intoxicating liquors.'"[32] Zapata and other Zapatista leaders craved no public office; they simply wanted justice for the communities that had elected them *jefe*.

Madero could not see the heart of the Zapatista movement or the need for immediate reform of land policies. A year after he took office, rebellions for land reform continued to undermine the stability of his administration; battles raged from Sonora and Tamaulipas to Chiapas and Campeche, the four corners of the country. Even so, Madero still did not see the immediacy of the issue. He calmly informed the Twenty-sixth Congress, "If Mexico could solve her agrarian problem within twenty years she could well be proud of the achievement."[33]

Twenty years, by Zapatista standards, would not be soon enough; they vowed to fight until land reform was a reality. The government, crumbling beneath Madero's ineffectual leadership and confused by the guerrilla tactics of revolutionary armies, responded with force instead of compromise. One veteran general, Juvencio Robles, took matters into his own hands and directed a policy of "resettlement," emptying the countryside of all inhabitants, setting fire to the pueblos, or villages, and sending evicted peasants into slave camps across the country. The pueblos of Nexpa, San Rafael, Los Hornos, Elotes, and parts of Villa de Ayala were all destroyed by Robles's forces. The peasants who managed to escape the government swarmed to Zapata's side, where they fought with bitter loyalty.

The Orozco Rebellion

While Zapatistas fought in the south, Madero's government was also being challenged in the north. In the state of Chihuahua, the same people who had fought in opposition to Díaz began to fight against Madero. Groups of cowboys, villagers, Indians, small ranch owners, and even bandits organized a massive anti-

In northern Mexico, Pascual Orozco (center) led an anti-Madero rebellion. The rebel's demands included Madero's resignation, improved wages and working conditions, and agrarian reform.

Madero movement guided by Pascual Orozco and known as the Orozco Rebellion. On March 3, 1912, Orozco officially declared his opposition to Madero, and on March 25 published his Plan Orozquista. The plan denounced Madero as incompetent and untrustworthy, and called for his removal from office. It advocated better wages and conditions for laborers, as well as the nationalization of the railroads, and, like the Plan de Ayala, called for immediate agrarian reform and the division of the large haciendas.

Orozco was enormously popular as a *"macho caudillo,"* or tough, arrogant revolutionary leader, but he was also young and gullible. His rebelliousness sprang in part from his belief that Madero had twice failed to offer him a position as governor of the state of Chihuahua. Orozco felt betrayed by Madero, and his sense of betrayal got the better of his patriotic idealism. Unlike Zapata, who was willing to die to gain justice for his people, Orozco was motivated more by a desire to get even with Madero and achieve personal power.

So when two wealthy landowners promised Orozco power, financial backing, and social prestige if he would lead an uprising against Madero, the young leader quickly accepted. Juan Creel gave Orozco

80,000 pesos, and Luis Terraza gave him 200,000 more, a fortune at the time: Both men aimed to reestablish a dictatorship in order to secure their own wealth and power. Thus, Orozco became a front man for antirevolutionary forces. He told his followers they were fighting for agrarian reform and better working conditions, but in fact they were pawns in a game designed to topple Madero's government and restore elitest policies. Worse than this, many peasants joined Orozco's troops without any clear notion of what the revolution meant. As one historian points out, "scores of officers under Orozco and Villa had no clear perception of why they were fighting."[34]

The Defeat of Salas

In Orozco's first act against the government, he took over the port of Ciudad Juárez without a fight in March 1912. Late that month, Orozco led troops against government forces at Rellano, between Torreón and Chihuahua. When Gen. González Salas, one of Madero's most trusted supporters, pursued Orozco with a strong and well-equipped army, Orozco responded by setting a trap. He filled a locomotive with explosives and sent it charging into Salas's troop train. The head-on crash destroyed Salas's train and the supplies it carried, and killed many of the federal soldiers. Men who escaped the flames were shot by Orozco's mounted bandits. The incident was a crushing defeat for Salas; rather than return to Madero with the bad news, the humiliated general killed himself. Thus, Madero lost a loyal and valuable ally.

Madero replaced Salas with Gen. Victoriano Huerta, who had a reputation for ruthlessly subduing revolutionary uprisings and who was known as "the foe of all rebels."[35] Huerta hated Madero, but Madero was in such need of experienced military officers that he hired Huerta anyway. It was another in a series of political mistakes made by Madero. As historian Charles C. Cumberland points out, Huerta's appointment "merely amplified the smoldering bitterness he felt for Madero and stimulated him to complete long-cherished plans to discredit the Madero government."[36] Huerta did, however, take his military duties seriously, and

Gen. Victoriano Huerta, "the foe of the rebels," was hired by Madero to help subdue the revolutionists. Huerta had his own agenda, however, and worked to discredit Madero's government.

succeeded in halting the rebel advance. He defeated Orozco's forces at the second battle of Rellano on May 23. By mid-August, Orozco had fled to the United States, and by October the rebellion was over.

The continuing revolution cost the Madero government both money and men it could not afford. By the time Orozco was defeated, the size of the federal army had risen from forty thousand to seventy thousand men, all of whom had to be paid. The government was forced to borrow 20 million pesos to finance the counterrevolution, which led to bitter verbal battles in the Congress. Additionally, the war had cost Madero whatever minimal control he had held over the army; now, Huerta's knowledge of military tactics gave him firm control of federal troops, even while his loyalty to Madero and the policies of the revolution was suspect.

Successes of the Madero Administration

Despite charges by the Zapatistas and Orozquistas to the contrary, Madero did intend to implement a modest plan of land redistribution. Ironically, Orozco's rebellion had prevented surveys in Chihuahua, where the government estimated there were nearly 2 million acres of federal land that might be redistributed. To that end, Madero formed the Agrarian Commission, which began small-scale distributions in 1912. If the reforms of the Agrarian Commission were negligible compared to those envisioned by Zapata and his followers, they nevertheless represented a huge change in government policy. Both expropriation of land from large

landholders and the restoration of the *ejidos* had been considered only by extremists before Madero took office; by the end of 1912, these policies were receiving serious consideration in Congress.

Madero also pressed for political reforms. So fundamental was his belief in the democratic process that early in 1912, when it was time to vote for members of the new Congress, he insisted that the elections be free even if those elected opposed his policies. By April, the majority of state legislatures had approved reforming and updating the national constitution, ensuring that the president, vice president, senators, and deputies would be elected by direct vote. This would make it difficult for state governors to control elections. Even though a handful of local elections were still rigged to support government candidates, the elections of 1912 were the most democratic in Mexico's history.

And despite the armed conflict that tore up the countryside during the years of Madero's presidency, the economy as a whole gradually improved. Production of oil, copper, silver, henequen, and corn all increased annually between 1911 and 1913, as did the value of the country's total exports.

Continuing Conflict

Still there was unrest. The Zapatistas never let up their fight for land in Morelos and other southern states. *Científicos* unrelentingly demanded governmental stability and support of their privilege. Railroad workers, miners, textile workers, and craftspeople went on strike, infuriating the business community. Meanwhile, the U.S. ambassador, Henry Lane Wilson, stirred up trouble by accusing Madero of creating a dangerous environment for Americans traveling or living in Mexico. According to Cumberland, "diplomatic correspondence indicated that no American was safe in Mexico, [and] that the Madero government was responsible for innumerable American deaths."[37] Wilson's exaggerated reports increased the tension between Mexico and the United States.

The press, too, hounded the president. Madero had abolished censorship of the press, and he dismissed its consistently negative stories as tests of its newfound freedom. But a host of opposition newspapers made it their mission to attack Madero on a personal level. Historian Ross notes that these attacks had nothing to do with Madero's political beliefs, but ridiculed him "as a spiritist, homeopathist, and vegetarian" and "for shedding tears in public. . . . Madero was even criticized for having taken a flight in an airplane."[38]

A New Rebellion

On October 10, 1912, Porfirio Díaz's nephew Felix Díaz launched a new rebellion, confined to Veracruz and based solely on his claims that the honor of the army had been trampled by the new government. He had no revolutionary platform to offer the people, nor did he intend to reach out beyond the conservative and military circles that still preferred a dictatorial form of government.

While former supporters of the Porfiriato welcomed Felix Díaz, he got little support outside Veracruz. The army de-

On October 10, 1912, Felix Díaz (pictured) initiated a rebellion to restore the honor of the Mexican army. Díaz's minor rebellion was quickly suppressed; the revolutionary was arrested and sentenced to death.

clined to act on his behalf, and conservative citizens could do nothing without an army. Federal gunboats in Veracruz harbor remained loyal to Madero and took up positions against Díaz on the outskirts of the city. Díaz failed to prepare his defenses. On October 23, Gen. Joaquín Beltran's troops entered Veracruz through the undefended railroad yards and met with easy victory. Díaz was arrested, court-martialed, and sentenced to death.

Conservatives in Mexico City protested Díaz's sentence; Madero ignored them. The president also, however, refused to interfere with the Supreme Court, which decided to stay the execution. In January 1913, Díaz was brought to the Federal District Penitentiary in Mexico City, where he promptly began corresponding with potential conspirators about a new coup attempt.

4 Huerta's Reign of Terror

From his prison cell, Felix Díaz wrote prolifically to Gen. Manuel Mondragón, a popular *científico* who considered it his personal duty to restore the ways of the old Díaz regime. The two men laid plans to oust Madero, then install Gen. Bernardo Reyes, an old, grizzled soldier and Porfiriato, as provisional president until Díaz could be elected.

On the morning of February 9, 1913, their plans were launched. First, Rodolfo Reyes, son of the general, was liberated from his prison cell by young cadets who had been recruited to the antigovernment cause. Reyes obviously knew they were coming; he waited fully dressed in the predawn, the cell door already unlocked.

He marched off with the cadets to free Díaz. Díaz and Reyes then advanced with seven hundred troops on the National Palace, which had already been entered by a corps of their men. At 7 A.M., according to their plan, the cadets were to swing wide the palace gates in welcome. General Reyes was to be ushered to the presidential quarters where he would address the nation, denounce President Madero, and declare himself provisional president.

The detachment of cadets indeed entered the palace as planned, and even arrested President Madero's brother Gustavo, but their inexperience prevented them from taking over the building. Gen. Lauro Villar, who commanded Madero's

---

Reyes Unmasked

In a report reprinted in Hanrahan's Blood Below the Border, *Gen. Bernardo Reyes is described as a man who cannot be trusted.*

"Reyes, whose name is being used to head the new revolution, is simply like a masque at a carnival, worn to cover the real faces. As intimately as I know General Reyes, I am bound to say that he is beginning to be universally distrusted because of his propensity to leave his followers in the lurch at the critical moment."

Gen. Bernardo Reyes (pictured) planned to take over the presidency with the help of Felix Díaz and Gen. Manuel Mondragón, a popular científico *and loyal Porfiriato.*

loyal city troops, took quick action. He managed to liberate Gustavo, and deployed his men along the palace walls to defend it against Díaz's rebels. As Reyes approached the palace, Villar's men called out for his surrender. Then they opened fire on the rebel troops. Bernardo Reyes was shot dead, along with four hundred others, including many civilian onlookers.

The price for this effective defense of Madero's government was high. General Villar was critically wounded defending the palace, and Madero was forced to replace him. Madero chose Gen. Victoriano Huerta, even though his loyalty was suspect. Madero was tempted to trust Huerta because the general had escorted the president safely back to the National Palace during the attempted coup. Díaz and Mondragón withdrew with their remain-

ing troops into the Ciudadela, a federal armory located in the heart of Mexico City, a mile and a half from the National Palace. From this bastion, they trained their guns on the city.

Huerta's Treachery

Two days later, Huerta began secretly negotiating with Mondragón and Díaz to plan another coup against Madero. Meanwhile, he pretended loyalty to Madero. Huerta's complex and treacherous plans began to play out.

On the morning of February 11, Huerta ordered Madero's troops to open fire on the Ciudadela. The ten days of brutal street fighting that followed are known as the *Decena Trágica*, Ten Tragic Days. Cannon shells burst across the city, and machine guns manned by both sides rained deadly bullets on anyone who dared venture outside. In accordance with Huerta's orders, few shells hit the rebel troops. Civilians bore the brunt of the violence.

The *Decena Trágica* marked the first time the death and destruction of the revolution had affected the capital city. Food and water became scarce, and prices rose quickly, forcing some people to resort to eating dogs and cats. According to historian William Weber Johnson, "Corpses lay in the street where they fell, bloating in the February sun. Persons dying of natural causes could not be buried; . . . some were loaded on two-wheeled carts, taken to Balbuena Park [in Mexico City], piled in huge mounds and burned."[39]

Inside the Ciudadela, however, the rebel generals drank champagne, unafraid of the chaos around them. Though

Huerta convinced Madero that the rebels were surrounded, in reality men and supplies moved in and out of the Ciudadela unmolested. It was in Huerta's interest to prolong the fighting in the capital. Each day, the citizens became more alarmed while pressure on the Madero government intensified. Huerta delayed, as well, to force the rebels to offer him more power and wealth for his treachery; meanwhile, he kept troops loyal to Madero waiting uselessly outside the city limits, and let federal gunners know that he did not want the walls of the Ciudadela breached.

Five days into the battle, Huerta committed a brutal act of betrayal against the federal government. In a blatantly phony attempt to beat back the men of Díaz and Mondragón, he ordered soldiers loyal to Madero to march down Calle Balderas, into the vicious crossfire of rebel machine guns. This suicide run was as close as Huerta ever came to attacking the opposing troops.

Ambassador Wilson Joins the Rebellion

During the violent days of the *Decena Trágica*, U.S. ambassador Henry Lane Wilson became actively involved in the drive to secure Madero's resignation. Wilson had initially approved of Madero's government. He believed that Madero would support North American interests, as Porfirio Díaz had. But as Madero's liberal sympathies resulted in modest reforms and demands for concessions from American companies, Wilson changed his mind. He made wild accusations against the Madero government, going so far that the U.S. State

Upset by Madero's demands for American companies to make concessions, U.S. ambassador Henry Lane Wilson (pictured) joined the growing rebellion against Madero.

Department eventually rebuked Wilson for his excesses. Still, he persisted, and as unrest and civil strife tore up the streets of Mexico City, he saw the opportunity to play a major role in the country's history.

On February 15, Wilson called together the ambassadors from Spain, Germany, and Great Britain. He described Madero as "crazy, a fool, a lunatic, who could and should be declared incompetent to sit in the [presidential] office."[40] He convinced the other diplomats to join him in drafting a letter asking Madero to resign. When the Spanish ambassador delivered their message, Madero angrily denied that the representatives of foreign powers had any right to make such a request, and vowed to die at his post rather than bow to foreign pressures. The president declared, "I will never resign. The people have elected me, and I will die, if necessary, in the fulfillment of my obligation."[41]

Representatives of other foreign nations supported Madero in his resolve. They felt the United States had no right to intervene in Mexican politics. Said the Cuban ambassador, "The intervention of the United States or the underhanded overthrow of Madero would explain the tortuous conduct and obscure words of the Ambassador. The revolution was no longer in the Ciudadela, but in the spirit of Mr. Wilson. Madero did not have to fear Felix Díaz, but the representative of President Taft."[42] In other words, Henry Lane Wilson, U.S. ambassador to Mexico, constituted more of a threat to Madero than did the rebel troops shelling the city.

A Final Coup Against the President

The *Decena Trágica* was taking its toll. Stunned by the fighting, a small delegation of conservative Mexican senators approached Madero with another demand for his resignation. He refused to see them. It became clear to Huerta and Díaz that they must physically remove Madero from office, since intimidation was not working.

On February 17, rebels told Henry Lane Wilson that he could expect Madero's removal at any moment. That evening, finally convinced by intelligence reports that treachery was afoot, the president's brother Gustavo Madero arrested Huerta at gunpoint. But the president, af-

ter questioning the general closely, was less suspicious and let him go.

The next day, February 18, Huerta sprang his trap. He sent rebel soldiers with Gen. Aureliano Blanquet to the National Palace, where they overwhelmed guards and took over the building. They arrested Francisco Madero and the majority of his cabinet. Meanwhile, rebel conspirators lured Gustavo Madero to lunch at the Gambrinus Restaurant, where Huerta's soldiers captured him.

That night, Gustavo Madero was brought to the Ciudadela, where a mob of carousing rebels tortured him, gouged out his one good eye, beat him, and finally stabbed him to death. Ambassador Wilson, who was involved in the conspiracy,

The president's brother, Gustavo Madero, was captured and tortured by Huerta's rebel troops. After being beaten and having his eye gouged out, Gustavo was ultimately stabbed to death.

then called Díaz and Huerta together to draft a document, called the Pact of the Embassy, that outlined a plan for restoring peace. The agreement acknowledged Huerta's right to become the provisional president. It also included a promise by Huerta and Díaz to do anything necessary to prevent the Madero regime from regaining power.

Wilson was pleased with the outcome of this meeting. The following night, Huerta and Díaz forced Madero and the vice president, José María Pino Suárez, to resign. According to the constitution, the presidency had to be turned over to cabinet member Pedro Lascuráin. Huerta followed the rules to give the appearance of creating an honest government, then forced Lascuráin to resign as well, putting Huerta next in line for succession. Mexico had three presidents within an hour that evening, and Huerta had finally achieved his dream of power.

The new leader announced that Madero and Pino Suárez would be allowed to live in exile, and a train was prepared to take the prisoners to the port of Veracruz. Before the train departed, however, Huerta canceled the trip, saying that Madero sympathizers were stationed in Veracruz, and could threaten national security by helping the ex-president reclaim the presidency. Huerta issued orders to transfer Madero and Pino Suárez from the National Palace to the federal penitentiary, but the deposed officials never made it to their new holding cells. On the night of February 21, Madero and Pino Suárez were shot to death outside the prison gates. Wilson accepted Huerta's obviously false report that the the two elected leaders were shot in random gunfire between prison guards and Madero sympathizers,

but all physical evidence at the scene indicated that the men had been executed without a struggle.

A Bloody Dictatorship

Huerta had finally achieved his dream of becoming president. He was able to take over parts of the country peacefully, simply by replacing governors with his own handpicked men. But in the north, a wealthy landowner named Venustiano Carranza, the governor of Coahuila, announced his refusal to recognize Huerta

After forcing the resignation of Madero, Victoriano Huerta (pictured) assumed the presidency. Many people rejected Huerta's government, believing that he had violated the constitution.

A Conspiracy to Overthrow Madero

In a confidential report reprinted in Hanrahan's Blood Below the Border: American Eye-witness Accounts of the Mexican Revolution, *U.S. naval officer Bayard Hale describes the conditions that led to Madero's overthrow.*

"[Madero] was by nature unfitted to the part of a tyrant; a little man, of unimpressive presence and manner, highly nervous, overwhelmed by his troubles, surrounded by incompetents, trying to be severe but yielding, Madero, at the end of his first year in the presidency, was in a bad way. The country was to a considerable extent unsettled; murmuring was heard from every side; the treasury was depleted, and a gang of grafters scarcely less audacious than the hated Científicos who had wrecked Porfirio Díaz's rule were in the saddle. In a land of settled political methods the case would have been no worse than that of a particularly incompetent Chief Executive at the end of a disastrous first year. In Mexico, it was fairly certain that, unless an early change for the better came, a popular revolution might be expected. But the movement that broke out in the capital on the night of February 8–9 was in no sense a popular revolution. It was a conspiracy of army officers, financed by a few Spanish reactionaries, in conjunction with Científico exiles in Paris and Madrid."

as president. On March 26, he issued the Plan of Guadalupe, which formally founded a new political party. Carranza's national constitutionalist movement claimed that Huerta had violated the constitution in assuming the presidency. Carranza put his troops under the command of Gen. Pablo González, and rose in open rebellion against Huerta. The Carrancistas, Carranza's partisans, believed above all that the constitution had to be upheld if the Mexican people were to prosper and live free of oppression.

In Sonora, in the far northwest, the state legislature also voted against Huerta's regime, and gave the military leadership to the young ranchero Álvaro Obregón, who would play a major role in the revolution from that time on. By the summer of 1913, federal troops loyal to Huerta held only the Sonoran seaport of Guaymas, while the rebels, now called Constitutionalists, were penetrating farther south, into the coastal state of Sinaloa.

Huerta made an effort to consolidate his power by arresting any state governor who was known as a Maderista. In the state of Chihuahua he abducted Governor Abraham González, then had federal soldiers

throw the Madero loyalist under the wheels of a train. Instead of buying peace, Huerta's acts gave revolutionary Pancho Villa the chance he needed to assume leadership of the Constitutionalists in Chihuahua. Villa had an old grudge against the new president; Huerta had commanded Villa during Madero's tenure, and had been preparing to execute him when Madero interceded on Villa's behalf.

Now Villa entered battle against the president with ferocious energy. Throughout the spring and summer of 1913, Villa fought doggedly against Huerta's federal troops, defeating them in six different battles. In one legendary battle, his men took over a train that was transporting men and supplies to reinforce the federal soldiers in Ciudad Juárez. They pulled into the heart of town disguised as allies, surprised Huerta's men, and captured this impor-

(Above) Álvaro Obregón (second from left) assumed military leadership in the state of Sonora after the state legislature voted against Huerta's regime. (Below) In Chihuahua, Villistas captured trains and fiercely fought against Huerta's troops.

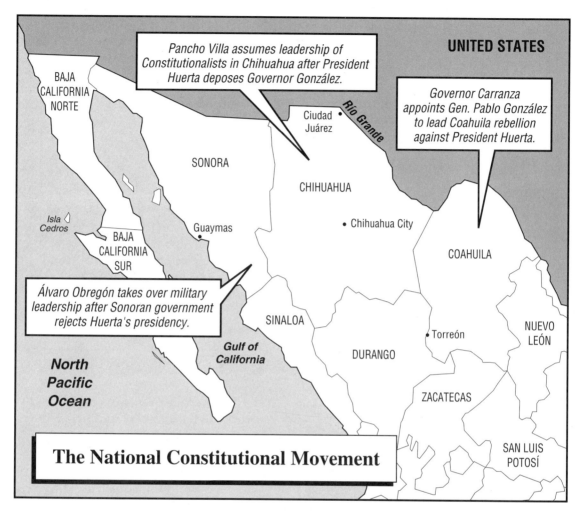

Pancho Villa assumes leadership of Constitutionalists in Chihuahua after President Huerta deposes Governor González.

Governor Carranza appoints Gen. Pablo González to lead Coahuila rebellion against President Huerta.

Álvaro Obregón takes over military leadership after Sonoran government rejects Huerta's presidency.

UNITED STATES

BAJA CALIFORNIA NORTE

SONORA

Ciudad Juárez

Río Grande

CHIHUAHUA

Isla Cedros

Guaymas

BAJA CALIFORNIA SUR

Chihuahua City

COAHUILA

NUEVO LEÓN

SINALOA

Torreón

DURANGO

ZACATECAS

SAN LUIS POTOSÍ

Gulf of California

North Pacific Ocean

The National Constitutional Movement

tant point of entry to Mexico. Next Villa took over Chihuahua City. The Villistas drove Díaz supporters and their families into the desert, took over the local government, then continued fighting to the south. By October 1, 1913, they had captured Torreón, a key railway junction in the state of Coahuila.

Villa and Carranza had been leading separate rebellions up to this point, and openly distrusted each other. But during this summer, they agreed that they were both fighting for more than the overthrow of Huerta. According to historian Henry Bamford Parkes, "they were fighting also to destroy the three traditional curses of Mexico, plutocracy [government by the rich], praetorianism [military dictatorship], and clericalism [a clergy wielding political power.]"[43] The revolution was beginning to take on a specific shape.

Meanwhile, in Mexico City, Huerta's government still failed to achieve formal recognition by the U.S. government. Newly elected U.S. president Woodrow Wilson and his advisers were suspicious of Henry Lane Wilson's involvement in Madero's death, and ordered the ambassador back

A Drunken Bully

Historian Charles B. Cumberland describes the dictator Huerta in Mexican Revolution: Genesis Under Madero.

"I was talking to the Chilean Charge d'Affaires [diplomat, of lower rank than ambassador] when Huerta and his Cabinet turned up. I made at once for Huerta and found him, true to his reputation, half-drunk. We three went to the sideboard and helped ourselves. I drank to the success of his future government while my Chilean friend stuttered something to the same effect. Huerta, on his side stuttered, 'D-d-dDiez [y] O-O-O-ocho c-c-centavos una c-c-c-cuerda.' Between these two inarticulate individuals I was a good deal perplexed until I found that all Huerta wanted was eighteen centavos to buy a rope to hang Zapata. After three or four glasses of brandy his Excellency retired with his Cabinet. During that night Madero and Pino Suárez were murdered."

U.S. president Woodrow Wilson (pictured) refused to recognize Huerta's presidency until the constitutional rights of the Mexican citizens were upheld.

to the United States in July. Additionally, American oil companies watched Huerta establish large petroleum contracts with Great Britain, and pressured the U.S. government to intervene.

In response to the concerns expressed by oil companies and other powerful interests, President Wilson set hard terms for recognizing Huerta's presidency as legitimate. Without this recognition, Mexico could not expect U.S. support, either politically or financially. In an official statement, President Wilson explained that his administration did "not feel that the provisional government of Mexico is moving towards conditions of settled peace, authority and justice, because it is convinced that within Mexico itself there is a fundamental lack of confidence in the good faith of those in control at Mexico City, and in their intention to safeguard constitutional rights."[44] Wilson added that he would only recognize the Mexican government if Huerta upheld his promise to hold free elections in Mexico, followed by absolute amnesty for all citizens. This meant that not only would Huerta have to run for election to the office he already held by force, but he would also have to forgive any crimes against his government committed by opponents during the course of the revolution.

Huerta also faced severe problems in his own Congress because of his displays of violent temper and drunkenness. More seriously, Huerta sent his troops to murder supporters of Zapata, and ordered the execution of his political enemies without a second thought. Finally, on September 23, 1913, Dr. Belisario Domínguez of Chiapas asked the Senate to depose Huerta, labeling him a dictator haunted by Madero's ghost. Such a haunting, Domínguez declared, was the only thing that could account for the insanity of Huerta's bloodthirsty reign. On October 7, the doctor mysteriously disappeared. When Congress protested, Huerta responded by directing his army to take over the building where the legislature met, arresting 110 deputies, and assuming dictatorial powers until elections could be held.

The United States Intervenes

These illegal acts obliterated any chance that the United States would recognize Huerta's government as legitimate, but Huerta went through the farce of elections anyway. While he was not himself an official candidate, Huerta manipulated

As tensions in Mexico increased, Victoriano Huerta (left) became a ruthless dictator. His violent temper and episodes of drunkenness caused his Congress to seriously doubt his abilities.

election results so that he was elected as a write-in candidate. Public outcry at this blatant dishonesty forced Huerta to declare the election invalid, but he announced that he would continue to serve as provisional president.

Woodrow Wilson sent a new emissary, John Lind, to Mexico City to urge Huerta to step down. Huerta, still in control, went into hiding. By January 1914, Wilson was advising the international community that he thought Huerta's regime was a failure.

Madness on the Streets: The *Decena Trágica*

An American citizen in Mexico City during the Decena Trágica *telegraphed a U.S. senator about the awful sights he had witnessed. The text is reprinted from Hanrahan's* Blood Below the Border.

"Now please look at some of these photographs. They were all taken after the fighting had been going on for at least five days, and after the corpses had been burned in piles. See the little boy with his chest blown out. See the good Mexican woman—the women are the heroes of this country—staunching the blood coming from the neck of her man. See the burning corpses of poor ignorant victims of a madman's caprice, whichever side their officers happened to be. See the machine guns set low on street corners and the men behind log barricades in the middle of our streets (all of these men were killed)."

In April 1914 he lifted the arms embargo against the Constitutionalists, and weapons were shipped to Carranza, Villa, and Obregón for use in their battles against the dictator. Even the firebrand leader Emiliano Zapata, still fighting for land in Morelos, hoped to get arms from the United States.

President Wilson grew impatient passively awaiting a Constitutionalist victory. When Huerta kept valuable oil contracts out of American hands, Wilson found a pretext to involve U.S. troops directly in the conflict. The crew of an American warship landed "inadvertently" in a restricted area of Tampico, and was arrested and held for almost two hours before being released with an apology. Wilson had the excuse he needed; on April 21, he ordered the seizure of Veracruz, a crucial port with access to oil fields. More than two hundred Mexicans and nineteen Americans lost their lives in the ensuing battle. Mexican public opinion against the United States turned bitter, and for a few days Huerta was hailed as a hero for fighting back against the invaders. Mobs stormed American-owned buildings in Mexico City, Huerta threatened to invade Texas, and even Carranza issued statements condemning U.S. actions.

Still, the U.S. support of the Constitutionalists worked quickly to assure Huerta's downfall. The armies of the north advanced steadily, led by Carranza, the self-proclaimed "First Chief" of the Constitutionalists; Obregón; and Villa. Zapata's armies virtually controlled Morelos, including its mining and agricultural operations. Obregón occupied Guadalajara, joined forces with Carrancistas under Pablo González at Querétaro, then marched on Mexico City. The road to the capital was open to the invaders, and Huerta dared stay no longer. On July 15, 1914, he resigned. A few days later he boarded a German ship and sailed into exile.

Chapter

5 Chaos for President

The struggle to restore democracy to Mexico resulted in the complete destruction of its government. In 1914, the national banking system verged on collapse, as the value of the peso fluctuated wildly, and government debts stood at more than three thousand times the amount available in the treasury. The damage to railways during the fighting had disrupted the distribution of food and supplies. Mills and factories had shut down or reduced production. Thousands of people who had once farmed or worked for a living now spent their days following revolutionary leaders from battle to battle. Even the weather was bad; for a second growing season, Mexico suffered a drought and crops failed. People now unable to grow or purchase food faced starvation.

On August 15, 1914, Obregón led six thousand men into Mexico City on the heels of the fleeing Huerta, and immediately set up roadblocks in the southern suburbs to prevent the Zapatistas from getting near the capital. Carranza, the First Chief, arrived four days later. Though not yet elected to any position, he established his government in the National Palace.

However, the fighting did not subside with Huerta's removal. The Constitutionalists had been united against the dictator, but once he was defeated, they turned against each other. In the north, Villa led an army of thirty thousand soldiers, the strongest military force in the country at the time. His boisterous men included peasants fighting for land, unemployed miners, cowboys, railway trackmen, and bandits, all fighting against Carranza to earn a little money and the chance to claim the spoils of victory. In the south, Zapata also refused to accept Carranza as First Chief, because the Constitutionalists had expressed no intention to redistribute lands to the peasants. Where the Villistas fought for money, more than fifteen thousand unpaid Zapatistas kept fighting simply on principle; they wanted their land back, and would die before giving in to a government unwilling to meet that demand. All around the country, bandit leaders unaffiliated with any of the major armies fought to gain control of villages, mines, and factories. The populace could not have been more divided.

A Disorderly Convention in Aguascalientes

Álvaro Obregón, now Carranza's general, was the only national figure who appeared

(Above) Pancho Villa (fourth from right) and his soldiers display their bountiful supply of weapons. (Below) Working under the direction of Venustiano Carranza, Gen. Álvaro Obregón (pictured) negotiated with Villa in an effort to bring peace to Mexico.

able to converse with all the dissenting parties. As soon as he had seen Carranza safely installed in the National Palace, he traveled north to consult with Villa. The two men hammered out an agreement that they hoped would bring peace to the nation. It called for a national convention and declared that Carranza would not run for president, but would serve in that office only until elections could be held. When Obregón returned to Carranza and told him about the agreement, Carranza stalled for time, arguing that the national convention should be held in Mexico City, where his troops could offer effective support.

Obregón again journeyed north to Villa. This time, the former bandit and revolutionary hero suspected treachery, and decided Obregón should be arrested and shot. Fortunately, cooler heads in the Villista camp prevailed. Obregón was allowed to board a southbound train, only to have Villa again change his mind and cable his men to stop the train. By this time, Obregón realized the extent of Villa's fickleness, and when he sensed the train coming to an unscheduled halt, he and his supporters took over the locomotive and steamed ahead into the night.

The convention proposed by Villa and Obregón became a reality despite this rift. In October 1914, delegates from across Mexico met in Aguascalientes, a supposedly neutral town. Obregón, Villa, Zapata, and revolutionaries from all over the country met for weeks, listened to long speeches by Mexican intellectuals, and plotted to decide who would become the next president. Carranza pointedly stayed in Mexico City to show how little he thought of the convention.

Though the convention was intended to end the revolution, it actually stirred up more trouble. One historian writes that convention leaders "hoped to prevent civil war by eliminating both Villa and Carranza; but they had no armed force at their disposal, and neither chieftain would take the initiative in resigning authority. . . . Villa's only constructive proposal was that he and Carranza should both commit suicide."[45] Despite Villa's

Caravans of Suffering

The revolutionary armies consisted not only of armed men, but of women and children who marched, fought, and cooked their way from battle to battle. This description of rebel troops withdrawing from Mexico City was written by reporter Francisco Ramírez Plancarte in 1914, and is recounted in Shirlene Ann Soto's Emergence of the Modern Mexican Woman.

"At the rear, singly or in groups, walked the soldaderas [women soldiers], burdened with a profusion of shoddy cooking implements and large bundles of clothes, and most of them with two or three children. They were following their husbands, whom they had not left since they had been carried off from home. Suffering had erased all graceful softness of line from their faces and all expressions of sweetness from their eyes, leaving in their place the august marks of grief and the sublimity of resignation. They were just starting the march and they already showed a marked feeling of fatigue and tiredness. It was a sad caravan of suffering. The women were miserably dressed; some went barefoot, most wore sandals and very few had rough, worn-out shoes. The children were half-naked, barefoot, filthy, dressed in rags, many of them with nothing to cover their heads, their little faces numb with cold and emaciated by repeated fasts. Their look was inexpressive, like that of an idiot. Many of them wept in a heartrending manner."

unpredictable sense of humor, the convention did manage to adopt Zapata's Plan de Ayala "in principle." On November 1 they elected a new provisional president, Eulalio Gutiérrez, a noncontroversial general from San Luis Potosí.

Electing Gutiérrez president was one thing, but persuading people to accept him was another. Even delegates who had sworn to uphold the decisions made at the convention felt lukewarm toward Gutiérrez, because he had no plan of his own. Carranza refused to step down, and was declared a traitor by the convention. President Gutiérrez quickly appointed Villa his chief general, and gave him the task of subduing Carranza's revolution.

Obregón initially supported the new constitution, along with its call for land reform and free elections, but when he saw the breakdown of the negotiated peace,

he decided nothing could prevent war. He thought Carranza was the most stable leader, so he joined him in his new headquarters in Veracruz. Within a week, Carranza's troops swelled as dozens of important revolutionary leaders abandoned Villa for fear of his fiery, erratic temperament. Villa and Zapata joined ranks against them, and once again the country was thrown into turmoil and armed encounters.

Killing and Plundering as They Pleased

By November 1914, Villista and Zapatista forces had displaced Carranza from Mexico City. Villa and Zapata rode into the capital city together, Villa in a khaki mili-

---

Shot on Sight

The village of Nexpa was only one of many towns which fell victim to the policy of "resettlement" administered by the federal government in Morelos, as John Womack Jr. describes in Zapata and the Mexican Revolution.

"Along the Chinameca River near the Guerrero border the [government] troops reached the little village of Nexpa. They found only 136 people still there, 131 of them women and children. After driving them out of their houses, they set fire to the ramshackle buildings. 'The residents cried and pleaded that the pueblo which had seen them born not be destroyed,' reported the *El Pais* correspondent. '. . . In the midst of the greatest terror and consternation the flames did their work, and a dense, black column of smoke rolling laboriously up the sides of the mountain announced to the Zapatistas hidden there they no longer had a home. . . .' All the Nexpans went back to Jojutla as federal prisoners, and stayed under guard in an army corral."

Pancho Villa (seated, center) and Emiliano Zapata (seated, right) joined forces against Carranza, Mexico's provisional president. Here, Villa, Zapata, and their followers pose for a photograph in the National Palace.

tary uniform, Zapata in silver-buttoned trousers and his trademark sombrero. But while the men rode together, their approach to the revolution was completely different. "The insolent [Villista] generals from Sonora and Coahuila quartered themselves in the finest houses and treated the capital as the spoils of victory; but the Zapatista peasants moved curiously and almost humbly about the city, knocking at the doors of rich houses and asking only for something to eat."[46] While Gutiérrez set about his constitutional task

of appointing a government, Villa's disorderly army of bandits continued with their wild rampages, "killing and plundering and enjoying orgies almost as they pleased."[47] Gutiérrez protested, but Villa, ever the bully, threatened him with military might if he intervened.

Villa slowly gained a large following of people who thought that Carranza was just another elitist dictator. By mid-December, Villa had persuaded fifteen hundred men to leave the federal army and join his band of soldiers. He captured Guadalajara

Support for Carranza (pictured) swelled after he published a list of reforms he planned to enact— reforms which included the guarantee of political freedom, the return of land to peasants, and the legalization of divorce.

and began attacking Carrancista troops all across the northern states of Mexico. At the same time, Zapatistas took over Puebla City, and continued to hoard the silver and redistribute the lands they had reclaimed from the hacendados in Morelos.

But Carranza gained strength as well. He explained his resistance to the convention by publishing a list of reforms he promised to implement. Not only would his Constitutionalist movement continue, declared Carranza, but on December 12, 1914, he vowed to guarantee political freedom, return land to peasants, tax the rich, purge the court system of corruption, and protect Mexico's natural resources from international export. Some of these promises were empty, others impossible to achieve in any case, but Carranza no doubt intended to follow through on some of them. He also formed an alliance with an ambitious young union organizer named Luis Morones, who later rose to

control the national trade union movement. Carranza even promised to pass laws making divorce possible, a popular step in a country which had been dominated by the Catholic Church, which forbade divorce, for centuries.

The Carrancistas also reorganized militarily. To raise money for a new army, they forced the Gulf's richest oil companies to pay taxes for military protection. Under Obregón's direction, twelve thousand soldiers were enlisted and organized into a skilled, well-supplied force. On January 15, 1915, Obregón's army marched into Puebla City and easily recaptured it from Zapata. Then he prepared to retake Mexico City.

Meanwhile, Villa gained support from the United States, from which he frequently bought guns and supplies for his army. On January 8 and 9, 1915, the U.S. Army Chief of Staff and a representative of the State Department met with Villa in Ciudad Juárez to discuss the convention. To the Americans' dismay, the temporary government set up by the convention was about to collapse. Provisional president Gutiérrez, tired of running a government dependent for support on the whims of the unpredictable Villa, was found to be secretly corresponding with the Carrancistas, and thus exposed, had to step down. On January 16, Gutiérrez fled to San Luis Potosí where he disappeared from politics into permanent obscurity.

The Struggle for Power

As Carranza moved more to the political left, Mexican reactionaries moved to support Villa, in whose disorganization they thought they might find a new road to power. The federal government appointed by the convention controlled only a few square miles around Mexico City. Officials there were kept busy dealing with food shortages and epidemics which plagued the war-torn capital. Outside the city limits, Obregón's forces threatened, and denounced Villa as a reactionary, antirevolutionary despot.

By January 28, 1915, Obregón had captured Mexico City. Carranza reentered the city a week later; he would stay in power for five years. Obregón, acting on Carranza's orders, immediately began levying taxes on merchants and clergy in the city, and recruited five thousand of Luis Morones's union workers to support Carranza in groups called Red Battalions. The start of World War I in Europe created a vast new demand for oil, and despite foreign suspicion of Carranza, his treasury swelled with revenue.

Villa refused to give up. He reorganized his troops in his northern strongholds to retake the territory he had lost. But in Obregón, Villa had met his military master. Obregón had studied the modern military tactics being used in Europe, and knew how to utilize tanks, barbed wire, and trenches to render Villa's army ineffective. Warfare had changed drastically in the few years since the revolution had begun: Some Zapatistas still fought with bows and arrows, while Villistas were armed with anything from muskets to rifles. Obregón's weapons were startlingly new.

In April, Obregón demonstrated the superiority of these weapons and strategies on Villa's army in the northern town of Celaya. Three times Villa ordered his ferocious cavalry to attack Obregón's fortified position, but men and horses were no match for barbed-wire fences and machine-

Shoot Us Both

Delegates to the national convention were desperate to find a way to remove both Carranza and Villa from active political contention. Villa offered this solution, recounted in the Memoirs of Pancho Villa, *edited by Martin Luis Guzman.*

"Felipe Angeles and some of my men had a telegraphic conference with me. Angeles said:

Sr. General Villa:

In his message to this Convention, Carranza makes it a requisite for his retirement from the office of First Chief that you also retire from your position as chief of the Northern Division. I advise you, my General, to accept this for the sake of peace. . . .

I answered:

I propose not only that the Convention retire Carranza from his post in exchange for retiring me from mine but that the Convention order both of us shot."

gun strafing. The battle raged for three days; when Villa retreated to the north, the Carrancista hold on northern Mexico was assured.

González Pursues Zapata

Carrancista general Pablo González engaged Zapata's troops in the south at approximately the same time. Zapata had retreated from Mexico City back into the mountain strongholds of Morelos when the city succumbed to Obregón in the early spring. Obregón sent reinforcements to González, who chased the last remaining Zapatistas out of the Mexico City area into hiding. Ironically, both the Zapatistas and Carrancistas claimed to be fighting for agrarian reform; the point of disagreement was Carranza's insistence that reform be accomplished under his leadership. According to historian John Womack, the Zapatistas "thought Carranza was an old *Porfirista* who would never carry out the reforms he had promised and . . . emphasized his personal responsibility for the recurring disorder."[48]

Gen. Pablo González, a staunch Carrancista, fought against Zapata's troops in southern Mexico. While pursuing the Zapatistas, González and his troops wreaked havoc on the countryside.

González approached the conquest of Zapata in much the same way Huerta had. He plundered and burned, while the Zapatistas hid in the mountains and attacked in lightning raids. González burned the few haciendas Zapata had spared, stole anything of value, and destroyed the sugarcane crops. Still, the peasants of Morelos remained loyal to their charismatic leader, and Zapata remained unbeatable by ordinary military means.

The U.S. government, warily monitoring turmoil in Europe and trying to secure its own borders, wanted to negotiate peace in Mexico. American business interests were tired of the conflict, which interrupted their profitable arrangements in Latin America, and, predictably, charges of atrocities against American citizens in Mexico, whether true or not, swayed public opinion. The U.S. policy of support for Villa had produced nothing but unrest. Deciding a change was needed, President Wilson simultaneously warned Carranza that the United States might intervene in Mexican affairs, and promised, on June 18, that he would recognize the Carranza government if peace could be achieved in the Mexican countryside.

A negotiated peace looked unlikely. Villa, after retreating into the Chihuahua

Carrancista soldiers proudly display guns that were captured from the defeated Villistas.

deserts of the north, resurrected his troops and fought yet another engagement with Obregón, this time at Léon. Obregón was wounded and lost an arm but the Villistas, short on ammunition, failed to vanquish the federal forces and again retreated to the north. And in southern Oaxaca, the conservative state government declared independence from Mexico. But the overwhelming weight of military might was in Carranza's favor. Throughout the summer of

Villa's Army Defeated

The battle of Celaya marked a major victory for General Obregón's Carrancista forces. Here Villa describes the battle in the Memoirs of Pancho Villa.

"At dawn my infantry began to move on the enemy in firing line; and Obregón's one hundred machine guns and the Yaqui Indian riflemen in the shelter of dugouts were firing with such deadly accuracy that we were hardly able to advance before we were decimated and broken; we had to withdraw to reorganize; again we returned to the encounter and again we suffered the same havoc; again we were driven back, once again to reorganize and attack."

1915, Carrancista generals won battles in the states of Aguascalientes, San Luis Potosí, and Zacatecas. Villa's troops began to desert in large numbers.

Carranza Ascendant

The Carranza faction, on the other hand, was becoming quite wealthy. Mexican exports had risen, especially oil revenues. Because the Carrancistas commanded the railroads, they were in a position to dictate crop prices to planters and small farmers. Labor unions, encouraged by the higher wages the Carrancistas offered and afraid of military violence, kept the nation's factories busily producing. In October 1915,

President Wilson and the United States officially recognized Carranza's government as the only legitimate regime in Mexico. Soon after, Carranza was recognized by Germany and Britain as well.

Now, Carranza began what he called "the reconstruction of the Fatherland."[49] He had a clear vision of the shape he wanted Mexico to take. Decisively, he raised taxes on foreign companies to increase federal revenues. Then he established a central banking system to manage the nation's finances and promote Mexican businesses. He believed that if the government could mediate labor disputes and help keep business running smoothly, all Mexicans would benefit. Prosperity, he believed, was the key to reestablishing law and order in a country disabled by civil war.

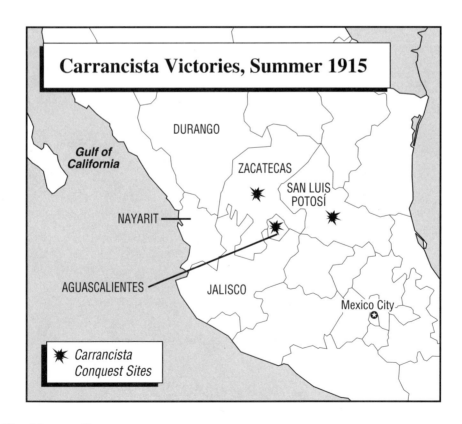

Carrancista Victories, Summer 1915

DURANGO

Gulf of California

ZACATECAS

SAN LUIS POTOSÍ

NAYARIT

AGUASCALIENTES

JALISCO

Mexico City

✸ Carrancista Conquest Sites

Gen. John Pershing's troops wind their way through the deserts of Chihuahua in search of the elusive Pancho Villa.

The reconstruction began forcefully. Villa rose again in Sonora to attack Agua Prieta, but Carranza's soldiers successfully chased the Villistas back into the hills. Villa continued to denounce the First Chief, so on January 14, 1916, Carranza issued an order to have Villa shot on sight. Villa continued to initiate raids, but with diminishing success. Arms and munitions that had formerly flowed to Villa from the United States were now cut off. Angered by this change in his fortunes and by what he perceived as foreign meddling in Mexican affairs, Villa turned his men against U.S. targets. Hoping to interfere with Carranza's connection to the United States, Villa stopped trains, stole arms, and even killed a group of American travelers. In March 1916, he invaded the United States in an assault against the tiny town of Columbus, New Mexico.

President Wilson, noting the increasing violence along the border and facing reelection, decided to send American forces into Mexico to capture Villa. For months, Gen. John Pershing led U.S. troops in a futile search across the deserts of Chihuahua. All the while, Carranza protested U.S. intervention; Carranza's troops even attacked Pershing's men in a display of nationalist force. Finally, with Villa still on the loose and Carranza unwilling to make war with the United States, Wilson simply withdrew Pershing from the country and turned his attention to the war in Europe.

Various rebel forces continued to operate throughout Mexico. But by November 1916, Carranza felt sufficiently comfortable as a leader to call for another national convention, this time to establish a new constitution for Mexico.

Chapter

6 A New Constitution

Venustiano Carranza cannot be viewed as a true revolutionary even though he played a large role in the events of the Mexican Revolution. Born to privilege, he grew up and was educated a hacendado. Though he supported the more conservative ideas (those that did not inherently threaten the economic or social hierarchies of Mexico) of Francisco Madero's revolution, including free elections, he did not actively advocate revolutionary policies himself, nor did he like men who did. Thus, when it was time to elect representatives to the convention to draft a new constitution for Mexico, Zapata and Villa were pointedly excluded.

Carranza's plan for the new constitution was merely to correct the language of the Constitution of 1857, to "purge it of the no longer applicable, to correct its deficiencies, to clarify its precepts, and to cleanse it of aberrations inspired by the selfish desire to perpetuate dictatorship."[50] He never believed that government should play a role in solving social issues of agrarian reform, labor legislation, or public education, nor did he see these issues as pressing. Interfering in those spheres, he thought, would be to control "individual initiative and social activity" that would convert Mexicans into "slaves of government's omnipotent will."[51] He

Venustiano Carranza advocated the creation of a new constitution for Mexico. The new document would revise and update the language of Benito Juarez's Constitution of 1857.

believed the free market system would take care of most of Mexico's problems. Still, he did advocate local autonomy, universal suffrage, a ban on the reelection of public officials, and legalized divorce. But

Article 27 of the Constitution of 1917 established laws pertaining to land reform and property rights. Of particular interest to revolutionists, the article ordained that the ejidos *that had been stolen during Díaz's regime would be returned to their rightful owners.*

the issues that most concerned the people—land and labor reform—he preferred to ignore entirely.

The Constitutional Convention opened in Querétaro on November 16, 1916. The two hundred appointed delegates were not all reactionary Carrancistas. Most had considerable political experience. They supported basic liberal ideals, and sought to prevent the church, which had a long history of using its moral authority to support the rich and powerful, from meddling in politics. Many delegates represented Mexico's middle class, like Luis Cabrera, an articulate lawyer and journalist. The radical faction of the convention was led by Gen. Francisco Múgica and his mentor, Andrés Molína Enríquez, whose writings on political theory had inspired the intellectuals of the revolution from the beginning. This faction enjoyed support from Carranza's immensely powerful and popular general, Álvaro Obregón. Thus, despite Carranza's elitist impulse to merely tinker with reform, the convention proceeded to put into legal language many of the aspirations and hopes which the revolution had embodied.

Article 27: Land Reform at Last

General Múgica developed one of the most important aspects of the new constitution, Article 27. This section of the document provided a new definition of property rights designed to undo the massive expropriations of property conducted under the Díaz regime. Article 27 overturned the absolute right of private property, replacing it with a new notion that private property would be subordinate to public welfare. In other words, if private property rights stood in the way of the people's basic needs, the people's needs would prevail. The new law resembled those ancient notions of property rights that had been in force when Indians owned the land communally.

Article 27 declared that the nation was the original owner of all lands and waters. Individuals might own property, but if national interests were not served by this ownership, the nation had the right to take over the disputed property. Additionally, all *ejidos* which had been stolen from the Indians during the years of Díaz's rule were to be returned to their original owners, and if this land was insufficient to support the local population, new lands were to be granted. Finally, federal ownership of its water and subsoil, including all oil and mineral rights, could never be alienated, or sold off. Leases would be possible, but never again could foreign companies or individuals lay claim to the natural resources of the country. This legally voided foreign titles to Mexican land, although no action would be taken on this issue for many years.

Article 123: A Magna Carta for Mexican Labor

Article 123, called the "magna-carta of Mexican labor,"[52] was designed to protect wage earners, all the people working in factories or fields to support themselves. Laborers had been subject to inhumane working conditions for centuries, so it was a significant change to limit the workday

to eight hours and establish for the first time a minimum wage. Double pay would be paid for overtime. Children under twelve years of age would no longer be allowed to work in the mines and fields for a few cents a day. Minors between twelve and eighteen years of age and women of any age would no longer be allowed to work under hazardous conditions.

Article 123 also prohibited peonage, the form of labor in which peasants were treated virtually as slaves working for abusive landowners. Wealthy landowners now had to pay their workers in cash rather than in scrip. This gave workers more control over where they could spend their wages, rather than being forced to purchase their food and living supplies at the high-priced, company-owned store, or *tienda de raya*. Additionally, the article stated that large employers must provide living quarters for laborers and schooling for the laborers' children. Women were granted leave for pregnancy with full pay, were guaranteed the right to assume their former positions when they returned to work, and received time off from their work while nursing children. Every business employing more than fifty women was required to provide a nursery.

In addition to prohibiting unfair labor practices in Mexico, the article gave specific rights to the workers themselves. Laborers injured while on the job would receive medical attention and compensation for their injuries. Unfair dismissal from a job could be contested, and arbitration boards were brought in to settle disputes between employers and employees. Finally, with government approval, the working class now had the legal right to organize unions, as well as the right to strike.

Vendors of all ages line the streets of this busy Mexican marketplace. Article 123 of the new constitution abolished unfair labor practices and established an eight-hour workday and a minimum wage.

Minimizing the Power of the Church

The convention delegates agreed that the constitution needed to separate responsibilities of church and state. Historian Henry Bamford Parkes notes, "The political activities of the church, the support which it had given to Díaz and Huerta, had shown again the need for drastic limitations to its power."[53]

Articles 3, 5, and 130 specifically limited the power of the church, which had held tremendous power for centuries, and still owned vast areas of the countryside. In order to minimize the church's influence, members of clergy were forbidden from running elementary schools. This was significant: In many villages, the church had been the only organized institution that provided any formal education for children. Now the government would take over the schools and teach a more objective curriculum. Another way government limited the church's power was by allowing only one priest to serve every five thousand inhabitants, enforced by requiring all priests to register with the state. Fewer priests meant less interference in people's lives. The church's huge tracts of land, from which it earned substantial income, and even the church buildings themselves were to be declared the property of the nation. Articles 3, 5, and 130 even gave the government the power to control the church's public functions; hereafter, religious ceremonies were allowed to take place only within church buildings.

Mexican women of all social classes faced severe legal discrimination in the early 1900s. Shirlene Ann Soto describes the situation in The Mexican Woman: A Study of Her Participation in the Revolution, 1910–1940.

"The wife has no rights whatsoever in the home. [She is] excluded from participating in any public matter [and] she lacks personality to draw up any contract. She cannot dispose of her personal property, or even administer it, and she is legally disqualified to defend herself against her husband's mismanagement of her estate. . . . [A wife] lacks all authority over her children, and she has no right to intervene in their education. . . . She must, as a widow, consult persons designated by her husband before his death, otherwise she can lose her rights to her children."

Marriage, which until this time had been an institution entirely controlled by the church, became a civil contract under the provisions of the new constitution. This meant that divorce became a possibility for the first time in Mexican history. Carranza had argued for years that people should be able to divorce, that women should collect alimony and manage their own properties. He knew that the impossibility of divorce meant that peasants rarely married legally in Mexico, because once married, even bad relationships could not be broken. Without marriage, women and their children were not protected if a relationship soured. With marriage, however, and without divorce, the situation could be even worse. One historian writes, "If a marriage failed, the wife, unable to support herself or to remarry, became her husband's victim, and was, by Carranza's definition, a virtual slave."[54] These problems had haunted the Catholic nation for centuries. Now, for the first time since Hernando Cortés had conquered the Aztecs, people were freed by the constitution to follow their hearts.

Philosophy Now: Action to Follow

According to historian William Weber Johnson in his book *Heroic Mexico*, "Much of the Querétaro Constitution [of 1917] was an expression of revolutionary philosophy rather than a precise chart for action, an expression of aspiration rather than achievement."[55] The new document suggested reforms that actually mirrored the needs of the Mexican people, but in some cases imposed such radical change that enforcement would be nearly impossible. Powerful members of the church would resist giving up their land and wealth, because to do so meant giving up their political clout. Labor laws would be impossible to enforce until industry itself became more efficient and productive.

Even so, the ideals of the revolution had been officially penned. Carranza officially endorsed the document on February 5, 1917, the anniversary of Benito Juárez's revered Constitution of 1857. Then began the long struggle to implement the new laws.

The First Chief as President

Carranza was not yet officially president under the new constitution. Elections for that office were held on March 1, 1917. Although approximately 3 million citizens were eligible to vote, the people were so cynical about the possibility of fair elections that only about 250,000 actually cast ballots. Of those, more than 197,000 voted for Carranza; the rest split their votes between Pablo González and Álvaro Obregón.

Carranza took office on May 1, 1917. The first legally elected chief of state since Francisco Madero, Carranza was to serve in office through November of 1920. Carranza's loyal general, Álvaro Obregón, resigned as minister of defense on the day Carranza took office, and appeared to retire from public life. As Carranza took up the reins of office, the nation held its breath, waiting to see what changes the future would hold.

If it had been left up to Carranza, very little would have changed for the Mexican people. When he was sworn into office with his right arm extended straight before

Venustiano Carranza (center), the first legally elected president of Mexico since 1911, officially took office on May 1, 1917.

him, he promised to "obey and enforce the political constitution of the United Mexican States. . . . If I do not do so the people may demand it of me."[56] He had accepted the wording of the constitution because it seemed politically expedient to do so at the time, but he was still a hacendado at heart. According to Parkes, "[H]e proceeded to ignore all the promises of reform which had been extorted from him during the civil war, and to govern Mexico in the spirit of a Díaz senator."[57]

As he told one associate, he "could not understand the constant harping on the agrarian problem because it was not the main issue in Mexico."[58] Thus, he dragged his feet when it came to implementing Article 27; mostly, he contented himself with ratifying land expropriations which had already been accomplished by the peasants

themselves. During the three years of his presidency the Agrarian Commission formed by Madero, which was the sole agency empowered to distribute lands, gave only 450,000 acres to 48,000 families.

Though it did not redistribute enough land to help Mexico's poor, the Agrarian Commission did make significant contributions to the cause. Agronomists and anthropologists from the commission undertook an extensive study of Mexico's rural areas. They studied the people, noted where they lived, the structure of their communities, the languages they spoke, the economic, sanitary, and health conditions of their lives, and the ecology and resources of the land that supported them. These reports were the basis for widespread land redistribution accomplished fifteen years later under President Lázaro Cárdenas.

An Historic Meeting at Querétaro

The Constitutional Convention of 1917 was more amicable than that of 1914, and accomplished far more. Historian Douglas W. Richmond, in Venustiano Carranza's Nationalist Struggle, *describes the variety of delegates in attendance.*

"An able group of delegates journeyed to Querétaro, and survivors remember the congress as one that raised hopes all over Mexico. A diverse group of individuals also came to view the historic meeting. Some clutched Bibles to their breasts while others waved *Das Kapital* enthusiastically. . . . Each received travel expenses and a government salary, and the atmosphere was friendly despite strongly held views. The deputies were younger, inexperienced men, a petty bourgeois group that represented rural areas. The most radical came from the northwest. . . . A majority of the delegates insisted that radical demands be detailed specifically in the new charter. They seized control of the key committees and enacted highly specific reforms which would serve as the nationalistic ideals guiding the modern Mexican state."

Carranza accepted certain provisions of Article 27 wholeheartedly. He energetically sought national ownership of the public lands that had been given away under Díaz. More than 30 million acres were reclaimed this way, a figure that makes the 450,000 acres given to starving peasant families seem puny and insignificant by comparison. Carranza felt Mexican citizens, not foreigners, should own their country, although he obviously limited this sentiment to wealthy Mexicans. "No more bayonets, no more cannon, no more battleships to be used to protect a man who sets out to build a fortune and to exploit the wealth of another country,"[59] he said, and his actions backed up this particular vow. He refused to allow Mexico to be drawn into the conflicts of World War I, refused to let the United States tell his government what to do, and, despite his desperate need for funds, refused to give up any of the fundamental rights of his government to obtain them.

While these attitudes may seem heroic, Carranza's reluctance to enforce the provisions of Article 123 put him in direct conflict with the country's growing labor movement. Although the economy recovered from the instability of the war years, wages were even lower than they had been under Díaz. In May 1918, labor leaders met under government sponsorship to create a labor movement, which Carranza intended to control. Instead, labor organizer Luis Morones, attending as a delegate from the federal district, used the convention to form an independent union called the *Confederación Regional Obrera Mexicana* (CROM). This group was organized much like the American Federation of Labor (AFL), whose leaders, Samuel Gompers and John C. Murray,

were friends and colleagues of Morones's. CROM helped organize Mexican workers against Carranza less than a year later.

The Death of a Hero

A major blow to Carranza's popularity came when he ordered and rewarded the assassination of the legendary revolutionary Emiliano Zapata. Zapata had remained a thorn in the president's side throughout the years he spent in office, largely because the principled leader from Morelos refused to accept Carranza as the legitimate head of the government. Instead, Zapata kept his troops in the field, harassing the federal forces in the ongoing attempt to achieve true agrarian reform. Not only did Zapata oppose Carranza within the country, he also caused problems for the president abroad. He sent representatives to other countries, including the United States, asking that they not officially recognize the Carrancista government and that they provide arms and monies to support the Zapatistas.

By March 1919, Carranza was desperate to find a solution to Zapata's opposition. "Order," he argued, "the resumption of sugar planting, the sugar industry and agricultural work generally, the revival of communications, education, and peaceful life depend in Morelos upon the utter downfall, the permanent absence, or extinction of Zapata . . . he is beyond amnesty."[60] He found his solution in a young army officer, Col. Jesús Guajardo. Guajardo served in Morelos under Gen. Pablo González, and was loyal both to his commander and to the Carranza government. But one day Guajardo made a mistake that threatened to jeopardize his career. Under orders to operate against the Zapatistas in the mountains near Huautla, Guajardo first stopped off to carouse in a local cantina. That is where his commander found him a few hours later, although the young officer tried to slip out the back door to avoid being caught.

Pablo González took Guajardo's dereliction of duty seriously, and had him jailed despite his talent and loyalty. When Zapata heard about the discord between the two men he had a letter smuggled into the jail where Guajardo lay, asking him to join "our troops, among which you will be received with due considerations."[61] The letter wound up in the hands of Pablo González. With Guajardo's cooperation, he formulated a plan to stop the rebel leader once and for all.

Guajardo wrote back to Zapata expressing a false eagerness to defect, bringing all his troops with him. As a demonstration of his earnestness, Guajardo and his men attacked a detachment of González's troops in Jonacatepec on April 9, 1919, captured them, and had them shot. Despite warnings by his advisers to be cautious, Zapata trusted Guajardo enough to set up a meeting.

Zapata set out in the morning, riding his prized sorrel horse across the familiar countryside of Morelos. By 8:30 A.M., he arrived in the town of Chinameca to confer with Guajardo. By afternoon everyone was hungry; Guajardo invited Zapata to a meal of tacos and beer. As Zapata and his aides walked through the door into Guajardo's hacienda, Guajardo's soldiers, lined up to look like an honor guard, leveled their rifles and shot Zapata at point-blank range.

Emiliano Zapata (pictured), one of Mexico's most popular revolutionary heroes, was killed by loyal Carrancistas who wished to squelch Zapata's resistance to the Carranza administration.

The hero's body was clumsily loaded onto a mule and taken to Cuautla, where it was dumped onto the pavement. For his treachery, Guajardo received 50,000 pesos. Giant headlines ran in all the major newspapers, proclaiming the end of resistance to Carranza's rule. In the hills of Morelos, however, a story arose that persists as legend to the present day. The man who died, some say, was not Zapata, but an impostor. The hero of the revolution, they claim, still rides the hills of Morelos on a horse as white as a star.

Chapter

7 Betrayal and Murder

Carranza became increasingly unpopular during 1919. Not only had he orchestrated the death of Emiliano Zapata, one of Mexico's most popular revolutionary heroes, but he began making decisions that drew widespread criticism. He slowed agricultural reforms, cut funding for popular programs like education, harbored corruption in his government, and responded harshly to labor unrest.

In 1918, he eliminated the Ministry of Education. Education had never been available to most of the population, but now schools that did exist suffered from money shortages. Rural schools closed, colleges had to cut back the courses they offered, and scholarships dried up. To make matters worse, public health standards often were not enforced, and many students suffered from untreated ailments.

President Carranza cut funding for education in 1918. Although schools were not widely available, those in existence suffered greatly from his cuts and many rural ones were forced to close.

An Unfair Trial

Desperate to win the presidential election, Carranza had Álvaro Obregón called before a military court to answer trumped-up charges of treason. Historian Linda B. Hall describes the scene in Álvaro Obregón.

"The judge, by the testimony of several witnesses, was terribly nervous; apparently he had been shaken when the two Yaqui soldiers who were standing at attention at either side of the tribunal had shouted 'Viva Obregón!' when the candidate appeared. By the testimony of several observers, the judge frequently went to the phone to get instructions and was heard to protest that he simply couldn't do what was asked. In his excitement, he even tried to smoke his cigar lighted end first. Obregón remained tranquil throughout, insisting that the court had no right to try him, as he maintained no connection with the military, and he consistently denied that he had ever met Cejudo [the nominal defendant]."

According to Carranza biographer Douglas W. Richmond, "Students healthy enough to attend school often encountered dark, shabby buildings that were inappropriate for public use."[62]

Nearly 70 percent of the nation's schoolteachers had received no formal training as educators, and Carranza demanded that these uncertified instructors be laid off. Schools began closing due to a shortage of certified instructors, and unpaid teachers went on strike. The public generally supported the striking teachers, and was disappointed in Carranza's refusal to expand educational opportunities.

People were also incensed by increasing political corruption within the Carranza government. Even while politicians mouthed the slogans of agricultural reform, land taken from the hacendados was not returned to the farm villages. Wealthy hacendados who were supposed to return confiscated property simply gave the land to their friends, or sold it, enjoying large profits. Generals who fought in areas with continuing unrest confiscated property almost at will, and sold it for personal profit. According to historian Henry Bamford Parkes, "A new verb, *carrancear*, to steal, was coined to express the most conspicuous activity of the officials of the Constitutionalist government." The government did not officially condone stealing, but they did little to stop it. Parkes writes that Carranza "presided, pompously and ineffectually, over what was afterwards described . . . as the most corrupt administration in the history of the country."[63] Small villages were pillaged by the very government they looked to for protection. Even the roads were unsafe, rife with bandits and greedy army regulars who considered anything they desired to be legitimate plunder.

Laborers also felt betrayed by the president. In 1919, rural wages dropped below the cost of living, and workers reacted by striking. Some workers complained that "their income had not increased since 1912, a situation that forced them to subsist on nothing but tortillas and *pulque*"[64] [a fermented cactus juice]. When workers struck for higher wages, the government intervened on behalf of the bosses, using violent repression against the strikers. For all of these reasons, Mexicans came to believe that Carranza did not support the masses.

Obregón for President

Venustiano Carranza had long realized that his former general Álvaro Obregón would be a potential rival. For though Obregón had seemingly retired from public life, he spent his days engaged in activities that showed his determination to become president when Carranza's term ended in 1920. Obregón expected that Carranza would bow to the inevitability of his eventual succession. But Carranza went on the offensive against Obregón's ever more public candidacy. In January 1919, he addressed the nation with a manifesto that declared that since federal elections were still almost two years away, no open declarations of intent to run should be made. Such early declarations, Carranza declared, were likely to cause trouble since the "anticipation of the electoral struggle causes citizens, especially men of certain political prestige in their respective regions, to extract premature promises before they have had time to reflect sufficiently."[65]

Álvaro Obregón had no intention of bowing to this ploy. He had spent too many months planning his campaign to back off just because the president wanted time to put forth his own candidates. His personal fortune had grown sufficiently, through sales of Sonoran garbanzo beans, to finance his campaign. He had regained his health, which had been in ruins after the shell tore his arm off at the battle of Celaya. And he had forged many alliances, both in Mexico and the United States, where he had toured extensively, even meeting (and impressing) President Woodrow Wilson. So when Carranza asked that no one make any official announcements, he complied and did not announce his candidacy publicly, but he

Álvaro Obregón was determined to win the presidential elections of 1920. His campaigning threatened President Carranza, who viewed Obregón as a serious rival.

behaved in every other way like a man determined to achieve the presidency.

In May, Carranza shut down all hostile telegraph operations in the nation, allowing only those messages that had secured presidential approval to be sent. The president hoped to cut off Obregón's communications with his many supporters across the nation, so they could not effectively plan his campaign or schedule meetings; however, Carranza did not have the power he imagined. The overwhelming effect of his presidential decree was to bring hundreds of offers of help and support flooding into Obregón's headquarters.

By mid-1919, Obregón had given up hope of becoming Carranza's official choice as successor, but he still hoped that demonstrations of public support would force Carranza to accept him as a serious candidate. Instead of waiting for a party nomination, Obregón formally declared his own candidacy on June 1, 1919. And instead of associating himself with one particular political party, he said that he had "no obligations of any kind, either inside or outside of this country."[66] He then invited the public to form a single new party, the *Gran Partido Liberal*, which would comprise small clubs across the country, all serving his candidacy.

Obregón, Self-Made Man

Obregón began to travel around Mexico by train, campaigning for broad public

Graft and Corruption in the Government

Graft and outright robbery were hallmarks of many leaders of Mexico's revolution, as historian Ramón Eduardo Ruíz recounts in The Great Rebellion.

"Accounts of graft and corruption, of 'revolutionaries' who publicly talked of *ejidos* for dirt farmers but went home to their *haciendas*, amassed fortunes out of public works, or took money under the table from businessmen and *hacendados*, were prosaic topics of gossip. . . . When a new governor of Chiapas assumed his post, he found the state treasury 'without a single cent to pay for the most urgent services.' His predecessor, a nominee of Carranza, had exempted his cronies from paying taxes, levied onerous dues on others, reserved public jobs for his friends, and saved money by reducing the salaries of lowly bureaucrats. He told newspapers what to print, controlled the courts, spent public funds on himself, tolerated monopolies in business so long as he received a slice of their profits and, as in former years, appointed the *jefes políticos*, supposedly banned by the Constitution of 1917."

Álvaro Obregón (center, wearing a suit) speaks with a group of Yaqui soldiers. While campaigning for president, Obregón traveled throughout Mexico; his gregarious personality and practical ideas won him public favor.

support. Although the newspapers ran stories about his heroic accomplishments during the revolution, Obregón downplayed his career as a military leader, presenting himself instead as an ordinary citizen capable of generous leadership. Indeed, Obregón was a self-made man. The youngest of eighteen children, he had been raised in the Mayo River Valley, Sonora. He had little formal education, but did complete primary school, and then studied at home with three of his older sisters who were schoolteachers. As a young man, Obregón read widely of literature and the labor journals of the time. When he became interested in agriculture, he displayed creative talent by inventing a machine that could plant garbanzo beans. Eventually, the machine

was reproduced and used on a number of large farms. He also raised beef for their valuable hides, and invested successfully in real estate.

Personally, Obregón was known for his witty conversation and charming manner. He loved to tell jokes and stories, and this gregariousness proved valuable during his campaign. He was a dynamic speaker, and gained public favor despite Carranza's repeated attempts to derail his political ambitions.

Obregón was practically unstoppable. He gained labor support on August 16 with the *Convenio Secreto*, a written document in which he promised that if he became president he would set up a separate labor department headed by someone in favor with the unions. He visited mines and factories, taking care to be photographed with work-ingmen of every description.

The police, under government orders, tried to disrupt Obregón's rallies. "In provincial cities Obregón workers were hanged and shot. Others were merely arrested on vague charges and held incommunicado."[67] But the repression had no impact on the crowds, who greeted Obregón on November 23, 1919, in Mexico City in record numbers. People from all social classes and walks of life turned out to meet the candidate. They waited in spite of a six-hour delay, which rumor blamed on an order from Carranza to deliberately keep Obregón's train from entering the city.

Carranza's Candidate

In January 1920, Carranza introduced his own official candidate to the electorate: Ignacio Bonillas, the former Mexican envoy to the United States. He was greeted by the people with derision; some even called him "Meester Bonillas," sarcastically ridiculing his too-friendly relations with Americans. Another self-made candidate in the race was Gen. Pablo González, whose lack of military success earned him the derision of cynics who called him "the only Mexican general who has never won a battle." Neither of these two candidates enjoyed a fraction of Obregón's popular support. At one party in Mexico City, a toast was proposed to the three candidates: "Obregón's name was greeted with applause, González's with silence, and Bonilla's with laughter."[68]

Carranza stepped up his repression. He hated Obregón, who had never looked

President Carranza selected Ignacio Bonillas (pictured), the former envoy to the United States, to be his successor. Despite Carranza's zeal, the public derided Bonillas's candidacy.

up to him with the respect and admiration he felt was his due as First Chief, and who, unlike Bonillas, Carranza knew he would never be able to control. At a rally in Tampico at the end of March, Obregón was greeted by a platoon of three hundred of Carranza's armed dragoons with machine guns trained on the public plaza. Obregón addressed the crowd of fifteen thousand despite this show of federal force, announcing to the crowd that there was not enough federal power in all the country to foist Bonillas on an unwilling populace. Although Obregón was harassed and followed by federal troops, he made his escape, declaring fatalistically, "whenever someone wants my death sufficiently to give up his own life, I will be a dead man."[69]

Carranza's last ploy was to try Obregón on charges of conspiracy. He had Obregón called to Mexico City to act as a witness in the trial of Roberto Cejudo, who was accused of treasonous activities. When Obregón boldly appeared in the military court, it quickly became apparent that he was to be the one on trial. Before the

---

"To Eat a Peaceful Tortilla"

Popular culture reflected the general feeling that Carranza's fall released the nation from war, and presaged a great rebuilding. This song, quoted in Frederick B. Pike's Latin American History: Select Problems, *said it perfectly.*

The People are very calm
As they watch this fuss and mess.
They say very calmly,
"It's family business."

The scramble to be president
Is one of our oldest haunts,
But to eat a peaceful tortilla
Is all the poor man wants.

Now the case is heated,
As we all can understand.
They're various the candidates
Who're trying to lead the band.

They've all got their program,
So that they can govern.
But what they promise us,
They'd better not give up on.

Let them remember what they've said
When they get in office at last.
Let them do right by the fatherland,
As so many swore to in the past.

Because the People have suffered enough,
And they want some consolation.
Today they ask for peace and work
And a president of reputation.

charges against him could be announced, Obregón and his loyal lieutenant, Benjamin Hill, disguised themselves as railroad workers and left the capital city concealed in a boxcar headed for the hills of Morelos.

There, despite the death of their leader, the Zapatistas still wielded a good deal of power. Obregón had been in touch with the rebels, and since March had been sure they would support his candidacy for presidential office. The Zapatistas, now led by Emiliano Zapata's old lieutenant Gildardo Magaña, felt they had a considerable unity of interest with Obregón's faction. Where Carranza was viewed as one of the landed aristocracy, far removed from the concerns of poor peasant farmers or urban factory workers, Obregón had actively solicited the support of both of these groups. His own past as a shoe salesman served well to secure the support of people who felt they could trust one who came from origins so similar to their own.

Outright Rebellion

Federal military officers in Morelos also declared their support for Obregón, who now began actively to oppose Carranza's government. Allied with the Zapatistas in the south, and with Plutarco Elías Calles, the governor of Obregón's home state of Sonora, in the north, Obregón had more than enough support from the military, the urban unions, and the peasants of the countryside to bring Carranza's regime tumbling down.

In Sonora, on April 23, 1920, Calles and his supporters issued the Plan of Agua Prieta, which accused Carranza of deliber-

ately ignoring his self-proclaimed principle of popular suffrage, and of betraying the revolution. The plan became a rallying point of support for Obregón. Telegrams poured in from sympathizers around the nation. Entire army battalions declared for Obregón, as did vast numbers of ordinary citizens. The few military commanders who remained loyal to Carranza found that they could not command the loyalty of their troops.

By the end of the month, rebellions against the central government had erupted in the states of Nayarit, Nuevo León, Veracruz, Michoacán, San Luis Potosí, Chihuahua, Hidalgo, Oaxaca, Morelos, Chiapas, Zacatecas, Tabasco, and Mexico. Carranza issued a manifesto asking the public to defend the government against uprising forces, but his plea was useless. On May 5, 1920, as Carranza presided over Cinco de Mayo observances in Mexico City, he received word that Gen. Benjamin Hill was approaching from the south, leading Zapatista troops. Obregón and former Carranza general Pablo González were moving toward the capital, as well.

"The Expeditionary Column of Legality"

Carranza realized his predicament, and decided to leave the capital for Veracruz, where he hoped to find refuge with his daughter's family and his old friend Gen. Guadalupe Sánchez. He calmly began issuing orders for his servants to pack up the family's belongings for the journey. But Carranza's notion of what belonged to his family made the evacuation one of the

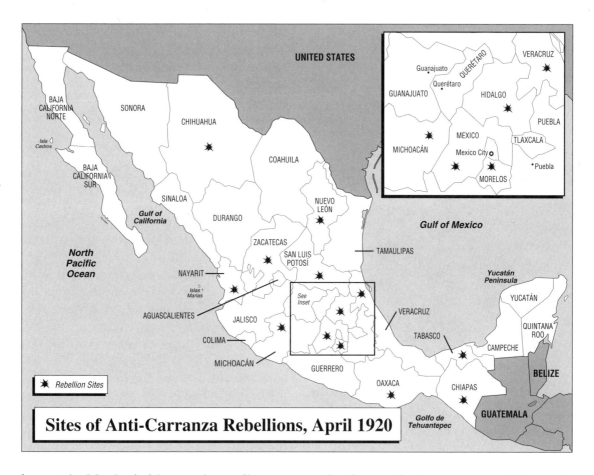

Sites of Anti-Carranza Rebellions, April 1920

largest in Mexico's history. According to historian William Weber Johnson, "The treasury was emptied of coin, currency, gold, and silver bullion, and the dies from the mint. Printing presses, cartridge-making machinery, and airplanes were disassembled and crated. Furniture from the National Palace was boxed, and the national archives were packed for shipment."[70] Additionally, every last loyal *Carrancista*, about ten thousand people, packed up their household goods and prepared to join Carranza in Veracruz. Trains were assembled to carry the mountains of packages, horses, and people.

Less than forty-eight hours after Carranza had ordered the evacuation, the trains began the journey out of the capital. The convoy was more than fifteen miles long; Carranza called it "the Expeditionary Column of Legality."[71] The trip was dangerous from the beginning. Several of Carranza's ex-generals led attacks against the convoy, and rebellious railroad workers sabotaged one of the locomotives by setting a loose train car full of dynamite in its way. Hundreds were killed even before the expedition made it to the state of Tlaxcala, less than a hundred miles from Mexico City. As the attacks continued, Carranza mounted one of his horses to lead a cavalry charge. The horse was shot dead from under him, but Carranza escaped unharmed.

As rebellions against his government broke loose, President Carranza fled Mexico City in hope of finding refuge in Veracruz. Carranza met his death on May 21, 1920.

Obregón sent a telegram to Carranza offering safe passage to Veracruz if the president would agree to board a ship there and sail into exile. Carranza ignored the offer. He received a second telegram ordering the evacuation of all civilians from the convoy within four hours, which he also ignored. When the diminished convoy finally reached Veracruz, Carranza did meet his former general, Guadalupe Sánchez, but not in the manner anticipated: Sánchez was at the front of the troops attacking Carranza's trains. Carranza, forced to leave the convoy, packed a few possessions, lit a bonfire with the national archives, and with a small party rode away from the train containing the nation's entire treasury: 3,733,704.50 pesos in gold, and 58,000 pesos in silver.

Carranza's Death

The Expeditionary Column of Legality now amounted to about one hundred hungry and disillusioned men crossing a rough and mostly uninhabited section of mountains. That they made the trip at the beginning of the rainy season did not help matters, and the men struggled to stay warm as they climbed toward the tiny, isolated village of Tlaxcalantongo. The village offered no food for the men, and no pasture for the horses. The rainy night promised to be a long one.

At 4 A.M. on May 21, 1920, the silence of the village exploded with gunfire. Carranza was killed almost immediately, shot in the head by his guide, Rodolfo Herrera, who claimed the president had committed suicide. The next morning, villagers placed the president's body in a simple wooden coffin and carried it down the mountain along with his final possessions: a typewriter, his pistol, his watch, and his trademark tinted spectacles. Some officials maintained that Carranza had killed himself; others accused Obregón of issuing a death warrant for the ex–First Chief. Circumstances surrounding Carranza's death remain unclear. But one path was now completely clear—that which Obregón would take to the National Palace in Mexico City.

8 The Violence Subsides

Shortly before Carranza's death, Álvaro Obregón rode triumphantly down the Paseo de la Reforma into Mexico City accompanied by forty thousand men. Although Carranza died on May 21, Obregón could not become president until he was legally elected. For this reason, on May 24 the Congress elected a provi-sional president, Adolfo de la Huerta, the man who had been designated head of the liberation army in the Plan de Agua Prieta. (De la Huerta was not related to the exiled president Victoriano Huerta.)

Three months later, on September 5, 1920, Obregón was elected by a nearly unanimous vote, despite rumors that he

Throngs of supporters fill the streets as Álvaro Obregón rides triumphantly into Mexico City.

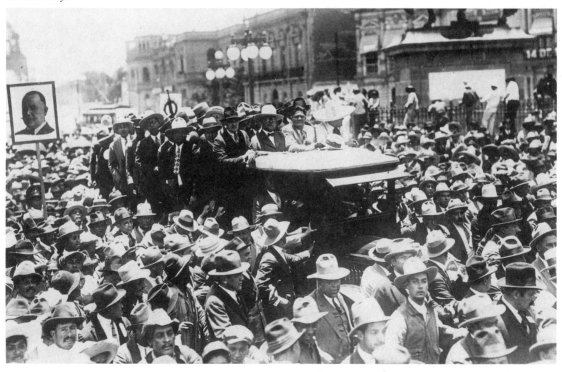

had conspired in Carranza's death. Plutarco Elías Calles was his new minister of war. The two men were fellow Sonorans. United by geography and by a certain political acuity, over the years they earned the title of "the Sonoran Dynasty."[72]

Agricultural Reform

Obregón began to institute some of the programs of the revolution neglected during Carranza's regime. Agrarian reform started in earnest; almost 3 million acres were distributed during the four years of Obregón's presidency, benefiting 624 villages. Under the system he set up, villages needing land applied to state agrarian commissions, which granted lands from neighboring haciendas. Each family was eligible to receive between 7 and 20 acres, depending on the productivity of the acreage involved. Landowners whose property was redistributed were paid in government bonds that were redeemable in twenty years.

More than 2 million families were eligible for land distribution; they lived in some twenty-four thousand free villages. But the 3 million acres distributed by Obregón reached only a small percentage of those eligible. Although Obregón recognized the necessity of land distribution, he did not believe agrarian reform was the most effective way to help the populace. He said the government should limit land redistribution in order to "avoid disrupting our agricultural production."[73] Both Obregón and Calles had grown up on

Álvaro Obregón upheld the agrarian reforms set forth in the new constitution, distributing a total of three million acres during his presidency.

farms, and knew rural Mexico from personal experience. They believed that improved irrigation and farming practices would go further to feed a hungry nation than dividing land into communally owned *ejidos*.

Thus, the government did not make it easy for villagers to apply for available acreage. Many villagers, unable to read or write, could not complete the complicated paperwork necessary to quality for land. To make matters worse, wealthy hacendados used their influence to intimidate villagers who did decide to apply for land. Landowners hired private armies to threaten applicants; others convinced the local clergy to speak on their behalf. Many priests denounced the agrarian program as theft that would earn God's anger, and superstitious peasants concluded that petitioning for land was simply not worth the effort.

Even those who applied for land did not always receive it. State agrarian commissions were often corrupt, lazy, or inefficient. When the agrarian commissions made grants, the agreements could be contested in courts, which required villagers to defend their applications in costly lawsuits. For these reasons, though 3 million acres were distributed by Obregón, 320 million more remained in private ownership. Most was owned by the same few wealthy families who owned it before the revolution began.

Education and the Arts

One of Obregón's most important achievements was the development of the nation's school system. He believed strongly in education, and in 1921 reestab-

During his four years as secretary to President Obregón, José Vasconcelos (pictured) directed the building of nearly one thousand schools, sponsored teacher education programs, and supported the fine arts.

lished the Ministry of Education that Carranza had abolished. Then he gave his secretary, the brilliant and philosophically inclined lawyer José Vasconcelos, an enormous budget with which to build schools. Vasconcelos took his job seriously, and over the next four years, built nearly one thousand new schools in rural communities across the country.

Vasconcelos established policies that would encourage future governments to continue promoting and funding education. In 1921, 72 percent of the population was illiterate. So, he sponsored the education of hundreds of young, idealistic teachers, more than half of whom were women. They were sent into remote villages to teach people how to read and write. Though paid salaries no larger than those of manual laborers, they were enthusiastic and dedicated. Historian Henry Bamford Parkes writes that they often worked "in mountain areas several days' journey on muleback from the nearest city," and were harassed by priests who opposed secular education. Schoolteachers were "sometimes in danger of their lives from superstitious villagers, [and they] often displayed the patience and enthusiasm of saints."[74]

Vasconcelos also opened specialized schools to train additional teachers, and those pursuing industrial or agricultural careers. He supported festivals of music, dancing, and art. He even began publishing inexpensive editions of the classics, including Homer's *Iliad* and *Odyssey*, which he sent to rural schools all over the country.

It was not uncommon for priests in the countryside to denounce the teachers sent to educate rural peasants. Secular schools were anathema to church officials. For centuries, the priest had been the intermediary between the poor villager and the world. Priests had, in fact, long taught small groups of children to read, but not enough to remedy the illiteracy of the general populace. The priests were afraid that if people could read and represent themselves, their reliance on the church's often dictatorial authority would decrease dramatically.

Art and the Cultural Revolution

Another of Vasconcelos's passions was art, and he began hiring Mexican painters to

Diego Rivera's political murals portrayed the turbulent past and colorful heritage of Mexico. In his paintings, Rivera immortalized Indians and mestizos throughout history and inspired a new generation of artists.

decorate the walls of the new school buildings. He hoped to see scenes from the classics brightening public spaces, but what he got instead, writes historian William Weber Johnson, "was an explosive expression of Mexican nationalism, first in terms of allegory, later as folk art and finally as epic history."[75] The artists he hired began to record the spectacular events of Mexico's history in vivid murals that are today cherished as part of the country's prized heritage.

One of these artists, Diego Rivera, was lured back to Mexico from Europe with a contract to paint a wall at the National Preparatory School. Rivera became the most vocal of revolutionary painters, and inspired a whole group of artists known as Dieguitos, or "Little Diegos," who wore pistols while they painted to protect themselves from critics who were offended by the political artwork. But these artists were safe in their political expression: Obregón protected freedom of speech and of the press. Historians, journalists, and novelists began recording their impressions of the revolution for the first time without fear of censorship by the government.

The paintings produced by the new artists of the revolution reflected a change in society unparalleled since the days of the conquest of Mexico by Hernando Cortés. For the first time in centuries, the people and activities being immortalized in the literature and visual arts of Mexico were not European, but Indian or mestizo, representing the vast majority of Mexican people. Finally, brown faces and eyes and hair stared down from the paintings that adorned the walls of the cities. Even the

This portion of Diego Rivera's mural from the Hotel Prado in Mexico City vividly depicts the diversity of life in Mexico.

form of the paintings, vast murals, sprang from the ancient indigenous tradition of decorating temple walls.

"A Nation of No Races"

This was one of the most lasting achievements of Obregón and Calles's rule. Racial equality was proclaimed, and while in social circles there was still a stigma to being an *indio* or a mestizo, in the world of government and business race no longer dictated a person's fate. Artwork expressed this new social consciousness outwardly; and in the minds of Obregón and Calles, it became almost an obsession. "Obregón and Calles became possessed with the idea of building a nation of all races, or rather, a nation of no races."[76] It was to this end that they supported education, believing it was the path toward a great social leveling. Thus, in the early 1920s, Mexico began to enjoy a cultural renaissance, even as the revolutionary struggle continued.

Diego Rivera's painting Children at Lunch. *While the revolutionaries struggled against the government, artists took part in a cultural renaissance.*

One of Obregón's goals as president of Mexico was to have his presidency formally recognized by the government of the United States. Porfirio Díaz had given away much of Mexico's natural resources, and Obregón knew that Mexico's financial stability depended on regaining control over its land, oil, and agricultural products.

At the time, Mexico produced one-quarter of the world's oil, and Obregón began taxing the export of petroleum as a source of revenue. In Article 27 of the Constitution of 1917, Mexico had reclaimed ownership of oil-producing land, but Obregón was the first president to enforce this provision, after first carefully explaining that it applied only to rights acquired after 1917, thus leaving intact all the concessions granted during the Díaz years. The U.S. State Department objected to even the minor inconvenience of taxation, however, calling Obregón's taxes confiscatory. Compromise could not be reached, and Obregón gave up trying to negotiate with the United States until 1923.

Adolfo de la Huerta (pictured) organized a coup against the government in 1923. De la Huerta fled to the United States after his attempt to overthrow Obregón and Calles was thwarted by federal troops.

Rebellion Against Obregón

In 1923 Adolfo de la Huerta, now Obregón's secretary of the treasury, organized a rebellion against the government following Obregón's announcement that Calles, and not de la Huerta, was his choice for successor to the presidency in 1924. Many prominent figures in Mexico's government hated Calles, who was strong willed and outspoken. One historian writes: "Obregón was genial, affable, gregarious—and Calles was none of these. Obregón loved to tell stories and jokes; Calles did neither. Obregón was regarded

with affection by the men around him and with respect by his enemies. Calles received awed respect from the one, loathing from the others."[77]

In December 1923, violence broke out. Guadalupe Sánchez of Veracruz and Enrique Estrada of Jalisco declared their support for de la Huerta, then rose against government officials by seizing funds and equipment, and murdering any who stood in their way. Hacendados all over the country took up arms against peasant communities, reclaiming redistributed lands. The military joined in, with over half the army led by commanders sympathetic to de la Huerta.

Obregón: Master of Populist Style

Álvaro Obregón was a master of political tactics, as this passage by historian Alan Knight in The Mexican Revolution *demonstrates.*

"[I]t helped to mix with the common man, dress casually, and display a certain plebeian camaraderie. Obregón, who claimed to like talking about nothing better than the diseases of horses, was a past master of this populist style. He dressed sloppily, stressed his poor origins and larded his prolific speeches with jokes and generous tributes to the common man. And it worked: people accosted him and greeted him in the street; on the stump he showed the same rapport with the women of the street, with the working men he met, and with the peasants in the country. While this was not necessarily phony, it was certainly prudential."

Obregón and Calles took to the field themselves, appealing to the people, who generally supported their policies, to fight on behalf of the government. In response, one group of militant peasants surprised Sánchez's army in Veracruz, preventing his attack on Mexico City.

Obregón, seeking support from the United States, agreed not to collect the taxes he had just levied on American businesses. The United States responded promptly by sending ammunition and soldiers to blockade the Gulf of Mexico against de la Huerta's rebels.

After three months, the rebellion was crushed. More than seven thousand soldiers had died on the battlefields. De la Huerta fled into exile in the United States, where he resumed his former career tutoring opera stars. Most of his generals were left behind to face firing squads as traitors. Fifty-four men, all former military comrades of Obregón, were shot to death in retaliation for their part in the uprising.

The End of Pancho Villa

Pancho Villa was another man who despised Plutarco Elías Calles. Villa loved de la Huerta, and called him "little brother." In early 1923, while the rivalry between the two men for the presidency was heating up, Villa came out of self-imposed isolation on his ranch in Durango to speak out on behalf of de la Huerta. "Fito [de la Huerta] is a very good man," he told the press. "He is one politician who would like to conciliate the interests of everyone, and he who does this does good for the fatherland. He is good, intelligent, and patriotic, and wouldn't look bad in the presidency."[78]

Despite his retirement from government affairs, Villa had been busy. He had bought the Hotel Hidalgo in Parral, organized a bank that provided low-interest loans to farmers, and even improved local roads. His temperament, however, had not lost any of its erratic, fiery character. He still exploded under the least provocation, still bullied and threatened those around him, and still possessed an imposing sense of personal honor. So, when he discovered one April Sunday in 1923 that the former owner of his new hacienda, Canutillo, had long ago sold off all the movable machinery and furniture, he was determined to

The popular revolutionary leader Pancho Villa was killed on June 20, 1923. Later investigations revealed that Plutarco Calles had ordered Villa's assassination.

right what he saw as a personal wrong. He summoned the agent who had organized the sales, and gave him thirty days to replace every item that had once belonged to the hacienda. The alternative he offered was death.

The thirty days came and went, and in a fashion typical of his character, Villa seemed to have forgotten all about his threat. But the agent involved, Militón Lozoya, had a longer memory. So, as Villa was returning to his well-fortified hacienda on the morning of June 20, 1923, with the ranch payroll in his car, Lozoya and eight men were lying in wait, each armed with a repeating rifle and a pistol. As Villa drove his Dodge touring car down the streets of Parral, Lozoya and his companions attacked. Twelve shots rang out. Villa's car swerved, then struck a tree head on. Lozoya's men ran out of the house where they had been hiding, still firing. Wounded, bleeding, with two bullets already in his head, Villa still managed to pull his pistol and shoot one of his assassins.

Villa's body was taken to the hall of his Hotel Hidalgo, where it was photographed and displayed for the nation. Rumors spread throughout Chihuahua and Durango claiming that the assassins had been paid 300 pesos each for the killing. Subsequent investigations revealed that Calles had, in fact, ordered the assassination. Those involved, after a period of well-publicized but meaningless punishment, were rewarded with lucrative government positions.

With Villa dead, de la Huerta in exile, and the populace solidly behind him, Plutarco Elías Calles easily won the office of the president when the election was held in the summer of 1924. The Sonoran Dynasty would continue uninterrupted.

Chapter

9 Reform or Oppression?

Plutarco Elías Calles was born the illegitimate son of hacendado Plutarco Elías Lucero and Doña Jesús Campuzano on September 25, 1877, in the city of Guaymas, Sonora. He took his last name from his stepfather, Juan B. Calles. His family lived modestly, though several of his uncles were distinguished political figures. A good student, as a young man Calles attended the State Normal School at Hermosillo, and then worked as a public schoolteacher.

But Calles's early career was marred by financial debacles. While treasurer of the Guaymas Teachers' Association, funds entrusted to Calles mysteriously disappeared, and although no dishonesty could be proved, he was dismissed from his teaching duties by the school board. His uncle then appointed him to the office of municipal treasurer, but again, a state audit revealed inexplicable shortages at the end of the fiscal year. He went on to manage several businesses that failed, then ran unsuccessfully for Congress in 1911.

In 1912, Calles was appointed chief of police in the tiny Sonoran frontier town of Agua Prieta. He supplemented his income by opening a bar and a gambling hall that catered to tourists from the United States. Although not openly supportive of the Madero regime, when a peasant laborer

Despite his diverse and rather tainted past, Plutarco Elías Calles advanced quickly as a politician, winning the presidency in 1924.

shouted abuses against the president in the town square, "Calles without further ado condemned him to be hanged by barbed wire from the railroad bridge near the town."[79]

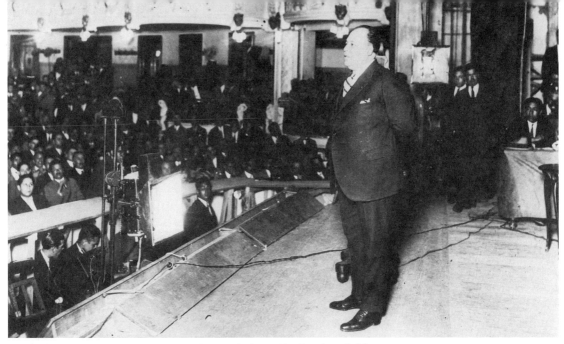

Luis Morones, the powerful leader of the Confederación Regional Obrera Mexicana, *addresses an audience of laborers. During President Calles's administration, Morones was named minister of industry, commerce, and labor.*

Calles had better luck as a military man. He joined the ranks under Gen. Álvaro Obregón in 1913, and soon became chief of the regular forces in Sonora. He successfully led troops against revolutionary uprisings on behalf of the Constitutionalists, for which Carranza promoted him to provisional governor of the state. Calles was fiercely moralistic, though hypocritical. As governor, the same man who had once owned a bar made his first act the prohibition of the manufacture, sale, or use of alcoholic beverages. Violation of his "famous decree Number 1"[80] was punishable by death before a firing squad.

Calles continued to prosper as a politician; he was only forty-seven when elected president of Mexico in 1924. Though Obregón continued to dominate the government during Calles's term, Calles grew

steadily more powerful during his time in office, and was responsible for implementing several major components of the new constitution.

Labor, Agriculture, and the Economy

Calles came to office claiming that he owed no debts to any political faction. But as soon as he became president, he paid special attention to Luis Morones, the leader of the *Confederación Regional Obrera Mexicana* (CROM). Morones, a "paunchy, heavy-jowled, working man's czar,"[81] was appointed minister of industry, commerce, and labor. In this advantageous position, he controlled a large and powerful segment of the economy.

False Socialists

The magnitude of corruption in the labor movement under Morones and Calles was so great that it did not escape notice even by foreigners. Here is an account by historian James A. Magner, found in Men of Mexico.

"Both Morones and Calles acquired great wealth; and, although theoretical Socialists in the beginning, they developed a native Mexican capitalism of a character and of proportions that could not but arouse national cynicism. After one year in Mexico, the ambassadress of the U.S.S.R., Madame Kolontay, declared that Calles and Morones 'are false Socialists and take advantage of the labor element merely as an instrument of their ambitions.' Morones' labor group, she asserted, 'is a bourgeois crowd directed only by personal interests.' As for Morones himself, she added, 'it is not possible that he can develop Communism in any way, when he is exploiting the working classes for his own advantage and that of other groups.'"

The constitution had granted workers the right to strike, but only if the government declared the strike "legal." CROM was not the only or even the largest union in the country, but Morones used his position to keep it in a dominant position. So, when other unions went on strike, he invariably declared the action illegal.

CROM strikes, however, because they proved the power of the union he represented, received his support. And to Morones's credit, he often helped union and industry find creative solutions to their problems, as in the 1926–1927 reforms he helped institute in the textile industry. This industry had been faltering for years, with labor disputes erupting continually. In 1922, 71 percent of the total number of strikes in the country occurred in textile-related businesses. Morones used his position as labor leader to bring management and labor together. They modernized the industry, adopted a uniform wage scale, and introduced the use of arbitration to solve disputes.

Morones and CROM pursued their goal to establish a single united union with incredible ruthlessness. They wanted every Mexican worker to be a CROM member. When strikes were initiated by other unions, Morones often brought out government soldiers to restore order. In the theaters, union representatives shouted down performances by nonunion actors; printing shops were either unionized or vandalized. CROM even proposed to unionize the prostitutes of Mexico City. But this zeal was not idealistic. Union officials built themselves fabulous houses, swimming pools, and tennis courts; they wore diamond rings and expensive suits.

All this power was attributed to a union that, while it claimed 2 million members in 1928, could show only fifteen thousand people actually paying dues. Much of the union's wealth came not from dues-paying members, but from bribes extorted from industrialists who wanted to avert strikes.

Although Calles's presidency was marked by this type of corruption, he did manage to secure some significant improvements for the Mexican people. A railroad line from Arizona to Guadalajara was completed by the government in 1927, opening an important route for commerce, and an ambitious highway plan promised to construct ten thousand kilometers of roads over a period of four years. Major irrigation projects were initiated. Between 1925 and 1928, 6.5 percent of the national budget was poured into dams and canals. Calles's administration also distributed 7.6 million acres to needy peasants across the country.

Crisis for the Catholic Church

Whereas labor leaders finally achieved political clout during Calles's administration, members of the Catholic Church entered an era of crisis. For centuries, the church had enjoyed immense power and influence in Mexico. Catholicism had been declared the state religion in the early Constitution of 1824, and it is estimated that the church controlled almost 70 percent of the country's wealth at that time.

Constitutional amendments directed at controlling the church's power were adopted first in 1857 and again in 1917. But in June 1926, Calles was the first president to begin enforcing the new provisions. Leaders of the church refused to

As conflict mounted between the Catholic Church and the Mexican government, federal troops charged into Zacatecas in pursuit of Catholic soldiers participating in the Cristero Rebellion.

abide by the Constitution of 1917, however, saying that it "wounds the most sacred rights of the Catholic Church."[82] Calles only grew more stubborn about enforcement. Hostility between church and state increased to the point of civil war, called the Cristero Rebellion, remembered as one of the harshest struggles of the Mexican Revolution.

Though Calles himself had participated in Catholic ceremonies at his daughter's wedding, he despised the power of the Catholic Church. He favored liberal religious groups that declared independence from the pope, and administered the sacraments for free. When he allowed one such group to worship in an ancient Catholic church in Mexico City, he provoked riots among devout Catholics who felt this use desecrated their holy space. Undeterred, Calles also enforced laws aimed at restricting the power of the church. For example, these laws limited the number of priests who could serve a community, and required active priests to be native Mexicans, over forty years old, and married. His government forced monasteries and convents to disband, and no longer allowed people to take religious vows. Religious instruction was forbidden in public schools, and all acts of worship had to occur inside church buildings. The churches themselves Calles had declared property of the government. And finally, priests were forbidden to criticize either the constitution or the laws that restricted their practice.

When religious leaders complained, Calles responded:

If God be the supreme significance of the good of individuals and nations, I do not believe that in this matter he is on the side of those who for more than a century have unleashed in Mexico domestic calamities, invasions, international intrigues and unrest of conscience.[83]

The Catholic Church retaliated by suspending all church services in Mexico after July 31, 1926. People rushed to get married and baptize their babies before the end of the month. Then the church urged all Catholics to stop buying everything except absolute necessities as a way of slowing down the national economy and pressuring the government to relent.

The Cristero Rebellion

The economy did slow down, but Calles did not, and in January 1927 the struggle became violent. In the mountains of Los Altos, Jalisco, an army of guerrilla Catholics organized uprisings against the government. Called the National Liberating Army, they were better known as Cristeros after their war cry, "Viva Cristo Rey; Long live Christ the King! Long live the Virgin of Guadalupe!" In thirteen states, the Cristeros attacked army garrisons, burned government buildings, blew up trains, killed labor leaders and Protestants, and then rode back into the safety of the mostly uninhabited mountains.

Public schools were a favorite target of the Cristeros, because priests were no longer allowed to teach. Some of the young schoolteachers recently educated and sent to remote areas of the country were tortured, often by villagers acting on behalf of the local priest. According to historian Shirlene Ann Soto, one young teacher in Zacatecas left her classroom when she heard a group of Cristeros approaching. "After being lassoed, she was dragged feet first over miles of rocky ground until there was almost nothing left for her friends to bury."[84]

The government fought back by executing people suspected of being Cristeros and stringing their bodies from telegraph wires along the railroad lines. In one case, the military opened fire on a congregation in a Guadalajara church. People who took no part in the rebellion were harassed by both Cristeros and federal soldiers. Churches were looted and destroyed, farms robbed, innocent bystanders killed. It was a time of intense distrust and hatred.

The conflict was also ruinously expensive for Calles's government, costing about 45 percent of the national budget. When the violence peaked in June 1929, Calles finally relented, and negotiated a compromise with the church. Laws restricting the church would remain in the constitution, but the government would not enforce them. Churches rang their bells and resumed services, and the Cristero soldiers went home. The bloodiest part of the Cristero Rebellion was over.

The End of Obregón

When Álvaro Obregón chose Calles to succeed him as the president of Mexico, his plan was to run for office again at the end of Calles's first term. He had persuaded the Congress to pass a constitutional amendment reversing the ban on reelection, so that a former president could be reelected after at least one term in which someone else held the position. The con-

President-elect Álvaro Obregón began receiving death threats shortly after he won reelection in 1928.

stitution had also been amended to extend the four-year presidential term to six years. A few other men ran against Obregón, and against reelectionism, but the former president won a second term in the summer of 1928.

Within days Obregón began to receive death threats, but he did not take them seriously. Several plots against the president-elect were organized by a twenty-six-year-old militant nun named Madre Conchita. She had been the director of a convent until the Calles government closed it down. Now she ran a clandestine Catholic outpost with a group of nuns who still sought revenge for the terror they had experienced as Cristeros. It was Madre

Young art instructor José de León Toral (pictured) conspired with militant nun Madre Conchita to assassinate Álvaro Obregón. Toral succeeded in his task on July 17, 1928.

Conchita who thought of the plan to assassinate Obregón; the young man she sent to do the job was a part-time art instructor named José de León Toral.

Toral became convinced that his mission was to kill Obregón and become a martyr for the Catholic religion. Following Madre Conchita's plan, he obtained a pistol and began shadowing the president-elect in Mexico City. On July 17, 1928, he followed Obregón to a restaurant, then sat in the back drawing caricatures in a sketch pad. He drew the orchestra leader, then moved closer to the head table where the government officials were dining. He sketched Obregón's assistants, then

Obregón himself from only a few feet away. Cartoonists were not uncommon in bars and restaurants, so Obregón's group took little notice. Toral held out his sketch of Obregón, who reached out to accept it. Then Toral pulled out his gun and fired right into the president-elect's face. Obregón slipped from his chair onto the floor while Toral continued to shoot. He died within seconds.

Madre Conchita and her nuns were arrested for plotting the assassination, and the trial that followed in November was sensationalized in the press. Because the law protected women from execution, Madre Conchita was sent to prison in Islas Marías for twenty years. Toral, however, was sentenced to death by firing squad.

Catholics considered Toral their martyr, and petitioned the court to prevent his execution. The controversy that developed was a bitter conclusion to the Cristero Rebellion. The government carried out Toral's execution on schedule, but as historian Shirlene Ann Soto notes, "Catholics made a final point when attendance at Toral's funeral was so great that police and firemen could hardly preserve order."[85] So the struggle between church and state had its final two victims: Toral, and the past and future president of Mexico, Álvaro Obregón.

El Jefe Máximo

With president-elect Obregón dead, the nation faced a crisis in leadership. Obregonistas, who had expected to rise with their leader into prominent government posts, threatened violence, even pointing accusingly at Calles as a possible author of the assassination. Had Calles attempted to remain in office, undoubtedly there would have been a violent reaction.

Instead, Calles reacted with a superb political move. When Congress met in September 1928, he called all the state governors and military chiefs to the capital. There he delivered an address proclaiming the end of caudillo rule, or the rule of one strong, popular man, in Mexico. From now on, declared Calles, the nation would be governed by laws and institutions rather than by personalities. He then helped establish the *Partido Nacional Revolucionario* (PNR), which was the forebear of the party that has ruled Mexico ever since.

Congress had the power to choose the next president, and with Calles's help, they decided on a man with allegiances to both Obregón's and Calles's factions: Emilio Portes Gil, a lawyer and the former governor of the state of Tamaulipas. When Gil took office at the end of 1928, Calles announced his retirement from public life.

In reality, however, Calles had no intention of giving up the tremendous power he wielded over government affairs. Many important men in government still owed allegiance and loyalty to him, although they outwardly served the new president. Calles became known as *el jefe máximo*, the supreme chief, and it was his influence and power that determined the

An Army of Women

Women often form the heart of a religious movement, and the Cristero Rebellion owed as much to the energy and dedication of the Mexican women as the revolutionary movement owed to the soldadera. *Shirlene Ann Soto remarks on the situation in* The Mexican Woman: A Study of Her Participation in the Revolution.

"In many places women made up the heart of the Cristero movement. They served as spies, organizers, and suppliers and carriers of arms, ammunition, food and medicine. The famous Brigadas Femeninas were founded in Zopapán in June 1917 by Luis Flores González. Their importance to the overall Cristero operation is indicated in a statement by General Jesús Degollado Guizár: '[The Brigadas] had become the principal means by which the Guardia Nacional was supplied with arms and ammunition.' In January 1928, the Brigadas obtained permission to establish headquarters in Mexico City and to take jurisdiction over the entire Republic. By the end of 1928 they had increased in number from six in Jalisco and Colima to more than twenty throughout the Republic. They had six branches of activity—finances, war, provisions, welfare, information and health—with over 10,000 members."

direction of Mexican politics for the next six years.

Gil ruled Mexico for only a year, until new elections could be held. During his brief administration, he oversaw the end of the Cristero Rebellion, granted autonomy to the University of Mexico, and, against Calles's will, stepped up the distribution of lands to the *ejidos*.

In the elections of 1929, Pascual Ortiz Rubio was the candidate of Calles and the PNR; against him ran José Vasconcelos, who had recently masterminded the flowering of education under Obregón. An intellectual at heart, Vasconcelos ran an intelligent campaign, which correctly pointed to the graft and military tyranny still controlling Mexico. He was a popular candidate, but when election results were announced, Vasconcelos won only twenty thousand votes while Ortiz Rubio, the party's official candidate, had more than a million. Vasconcelos declared the election

was fraud, but to no avail. When Ortiz Rubio took office, Vasconcelos, the man who had masterminded Mexico's flourishing literacy and cultural arts programs, was forced into exile.

Ortiz Rubio's presidency was even more of a sham than that of Gil. Calles lived in luxury in Cuernavaca, on the Street of the Forty Thieves, but he still ran the government by telephone. In September 1932, when Ortiz Rubio attempted to fire a few men who held favor with *el jefe máximo*, Calles informed the press that the president had resigned. Ortiz Rubio, hearing the news, found it prudent to agree, and stepped down.

A Millionaire President

Ortiz Rubio was succeeded by yet another of Calles's puppets, Abelardo Rodríguez,

---

Cristeros Whipped into Submission

The Cristero Rebellion brought out the kind of savagery that often accompanies strongly held sentiments, as this account by James A. Magner in Men of Mexico *shows.*

"A particularly scandalous, although typical, scene occurred, as a result of the order of the Secretary of the Interior, February 22, 1926, to close the popular church of the Sagrada Familia (Holy Family) in Mexico City and to arrest the priests in charge. Three thousand parishioners, including many of the most respected persons in the capital, formed a cordon about the church, and when pistol shots of the police failed to disperse the gathering, the fire department was sent to direct its hose indiscriminately against the men and women. To complete the tragic spectacle, mounted police rode upon the crowd and whipped it into submission."

Supported by former president Calles and the Partido Nacional Revolucionario, *Pascual Ortiz Rubio (pictured) was elected president of Mexico in 1929.*

the first millionaire to hold the office of president since the revolution started, and the first whose fortune originated in gambling houses.

During the years that he controlled Mexico from behind the scenes, Calles became more and more conservative. He backed fascist street fighters, called the Gold Shirts, who fought against Mexico's Jews and Bolsheviks, and put an end to anything beyond the mere appearance of land reform. He even repudiated his earlier agreements with labor, becoming by the 1930s a foe to the unions he had once supported.

In 1934, Calles recommended that the popular revolutionary general and governor of Michoacán, Lázaro Cárdenas, become the next president of Mexico. Calles felt pressured by a younger generation of revolutionaires who wanted to revive and extend the ideals of the revolution, and he thought Cárdenas would appease this group while still allowing *el jefe máximo* to rule. To the public, Calles announced: "Twenty-one years of friendship between General Cárdenas and me cannot be fruitless. This friendship, each day made closer in the struggle for the principles and the postulates of the Revolution, binds us two together with firm and indestructible ties."[86] As it turned out, however, he was sorely mistaken.

10 Cautious Progress

The official PNR candidate for president in 1934 was a young man with both Spanish and Tarascan-Indian ancestry. Lázaro Cárdenas y del Rio was one of eight children, born in 1895 to a poor family that could only offer their son an elementary

Before winning the presidency, Lázaro Cárdenas y del Rio had spent most of his life fighting in the revolution. During his term in office, Cárdenas worked to strengthen Mexico's economy and improve social conditions.

school education. When he was eleven, he began working to support the family. In 1913, he joined revolutionaries fighting to overthrow Victoriano Huerta. By 1920, he was a brigadier general, and joined Obregón and Calles in overthrowing Carranza. By the time Cárdenas accepted the nomination to run for president, he had spent most of his life fighting in the revolution, and he believed deeply in its popular ideals.

Cárdenas's election was virtually assured by the support of Calles. Even so, he traveled more than sixteen thousand miles of Mexican territory by train, horseback, and on foot, speaking with people from every walk of life, explaining his Six-Year Plan in practical terms. He said that his plan would build upon Calles's work, "to make Mexico a strong country on solid foundations, in this era in which the people of the world are locked in an economic-social struggle for improved conditions to gain genuine prosperity for all workmen and their homes."[87]

The End of *el Jefe Máximo*

On July 1, 1934, Cárdenas won 80 percent of the vote; he was inaugurated the follow-

Cárdenas Gives Back the *Ejidos*

Whereas other presidents delayed agrarian reform, Lázaro Cárdenas was determined to see the people finally get the land they had fought for over so many years. John Womack Jr. recounts one incident in Zapata and the Mexican Revolution.

"It so happened that the [expropriated] fields were among the richest in Anenecuilco's *ejido*. They were fields Anenecuilco had always held title to, as one of the cooperative's leading generals, Maurilio Mejía, must have known. Besides, the village had won the fields 'definitively' from Hospital hacienda in 1923. . . . Soon the generals sent out crews to fence in the land.

On November 29, 1934, [*ejidal* representative Francisco Franco] did file again for restitution. Then when the generals accused him of rebellion against local officials and initiated a private hunt for him, he fled with the documents [proving ownership by the *ejido*] into the hills. He spent several months a jump ahead of death, writing when he could to various authorities. . . .

Eventually Franco's pleas came to the attention of the new President, Lázaro Cárdenas, who had revived radical agrarianism as a national policy. And on June 29, 1935, astoundingly, the President arrived in Anenecuilco. In public proceedings he declared the generals expropriated, the pueblo entitled to the fields in question, as well as the cooperative's farm machinery, and Francisco Franco guaranteed against political abuse."

ing November. But since he was Calles's handpicked candidate, government officials and the public assumed Calles was still controlling the office. Calles himself assumed this was so, especially after Cárdenas accepted Calles's assignments for cabinet members.

But as soon as Cárdenas took office, he busied himself fulfilling campaign promises, and rarely consulted his cabinet. Furthermore, he closed down the illegal gambling houses where Calles's friends collected their fortunes. But most insult-ing to Calles was Cárdenas's attitude toward labor strikes. Not only did the new president permit them, but he sympathized with the workers, saying that it was time for Mexican labor to be paid fairly.

Calles was offended, and worried about his loss of power. In an attempt to control Cárdenas, Calles tried to stir up a religious uprising among Catholics. He sent government officials still loyal to the himself around the country destroying churches and imposing restrictions on clergy. In the fall of 1935, under Calles's

Plutarco Calles's control over governmental affairs ended when President Cárdenas took office. Calles (pictured) was forced into exile in 1936 for plotting against the government.

of blood, Cárdenas was able to neutralize the power of a man who had ruled Mexico for over a decade.

In April 1936, Calles and his old friend and ally, CROM leader Luis Morones, were caught hoarding ammunition and accused of plotting against the government. In a graceful display of power, Cárdenas had the two men arrested and forced onto a plane bound for Texas. Press photos of the event show Calles debarking the plane into exile carrying a copy of Adolf Hitler's racist autobiography, *Mein Kampf.*

A New Style of Leadership

Cárdenas displayed a conspicuously different style of leadership than his predecessors. He showed up to work early in the morning wearing a plain suit, and told the buglers to quit announcing his arrival with their formal fanfare. He demanded that the presidential portraits be taken down from the palace walls. He was a modest, soft-spoken man who took his job seriously, and his regime is still regarded as one of the most radical in Mexican history.

What made his administration so different? Cárdenas respected the Constitution of 1917, and tried to implement not only its letter, but also its intent. He believed that Mexicans had suffered too long, and deserved to have their civil rights protected. People sensed this change, and began exercising their rights, even demanding them. Organized workers struck without fear of government repression. Feminist movements pushed for equal rights. Controversial subjects like sex education, once forbidden by the

direction, the government closed 130 churches, and a resolution was drawn up suggesting that the entire Catholic hierarchy be exiled from the country. Some states outlawed church services altogether.

Although Cárdenas was not particularly religious, he tolerated Catholicism more than Calles. The new president was willing to negotiate with church leaders, and the uprisings settled down. Calles then attempted to gain popular support by denouncing Cárdenas as a communist; to the surprise of *el jefe máximo,* Cárdenas responded by dismissing the Calles-appointed cabinet.

At this point, Cárdenas assumed a full offensive against his former ally. He appointed cabinet members who supported him instead of Calles, and let labor and peasant revolts remove from power any Calles supporters remaining in state governments. Thus, without shedding a drop

"I am a Peasant Myself"

According to Frederick B. Pike in Latin American History, *President Cárdenas was popular in part because of his habit of traveling extensively and spending time in every tiny hamlet along the way, where he listened intently to the concerns of the local people.*

"'Hurry, hurry, the President of the Republic is coming!' And there he went, running and running. Now, Chico is no fool, he has a good head. By that time I was running too. Where was the President? He had to come through the dirt road on horseback. We saw a mob of people there and it was really he, it was President Lázaro Cárdenas, and we came running up. . . .

Then President Cárdenas said that the next week or the following one, the highway would be started. 'Don't worry,' he said, 'I am going to build a highway for you.' And immediately everyone drank to that. Well, the municipal president didn't know what to give him. What was he going to give him when he was taken by surprise like that? So he sent for some rolls, filled them with sausage meat, and offered them to the visitors. 'Go ahead Mr. President,' he said. 'This is all we could improvise.'

'It doesn't matter. This is fine,' Cárdenas said. 'I am a peasant myself.' And he picked up one of the rolls with sausage and ate it."

President Lázaro Cárdenas earnestly listens to the concerns of people he meets on the street while touring Mexico.

church, were encouraged for children in public schools.

Fiscally, Cárdenas reduced the amount of federal money spent on bureaucratic expenses from 63 percent of the overall budget to 44 percent. Thirty-eight percent of the budget funded highways, irrigation projects, and other economic developmental projects; 18 percent was spent on public health and education. His efforts to maintain the country's financial growth worked, and Mexico's manufacturing industries began once again to prosper.

Cárdenas also reduced the authority of the federal army. He wanted the military to function as a nonpolitical entity, serving the country's overall interests rather than representing only the ideals of the presiding administration. Generals sympathetic to Calles were retired, and soldiers were put to work repairing roads, digging irrigation ditches, rebuilding schools, and, in general, cleaning up after years of destruction wrought by civil war. Obsolete military hardware was given to farmers to convert into agricultural equipment. This perhaps more than anything else signaled that the Mexican Revolution was coming to a close.

Redistribution of Land

Many of the revolutionary presidents supported small, independent farmers, but Cárdenas preferred the *ejido* system. Each *ejido* would be owned by the nation, but farmed by the indigenous population of a region. He believed that redistributing land this way would encourage agriculture, as well as the cultural development

---

Women Suffrage a Basic Duty

In 1938, Cárdenas drafted a constitutional amendment that gave women the right to vote. The following passage is from his address to Congress on September 1, 1939, and recounted by Shirlene Ann Soto in Emergence of the Modern Mexican Woman.

"From the very beginning of my term I have been urging that the grave injustice be rectified that cheats Mexican women of substantial rights while, on the other hand, it imposes upon them all the obligations of citizenship. Suffrage in Mexico should be made complete by giving women the right to vote. Otherwise, the electoral function remains incomplete. . . . Although the idea commonly prevails that women's suffrage, if enacted, will be accompanied by problems of a reactionary nature, this should not prevent the enactment of the measure, for it is one of our basic duties to organize and guide along channels that are favorable to the nation, the fundamental functions of the sovereign prerogatives of the people."

Workers could strike without fear of government intervention during Cárdenas's presidency. These Mexican strikers defiantly stand outside of the Ford Motor Company.

of people who had lived on the land for thousands of years.

To those being forced to give up their farms for redistribution, Cárdenas said: "It would be of high morality and true sympathy for the interests of the country if Mexicans would be willing to forego the indemnity which might be due them by the seizure of the lands."[88] In fact, the debt was overlooked completely. Peasants were simply given back the land of their ancestors.

During his six-year term, Cárdenas distributed more land than had been distributed during all the years of the revolution. Nearly 50 million acres were given to 11,347 *ejidos*, which supported a total of 771,640 families. He also created the National Ejido Credit Bank, which provided loans to collective farmers, or *ejidatarios*.

In 1938, the *Confederación Nacional Campesina*, or National Campesino Confederation (CNC), was established, with membership mandatory for every *ejidatario*. According to historian Frank R. Brandenburg, "a quarter of a century after Cárdenas established the *ejidatario* central it persisted, with only minor alterations . . . , as the largest labor confederation in Mexican agriculture, possessing a membership of more than two million."[89]

Labor, the CTM, and the PRM

Cárdenas recognized early in his term that he would find loyal support among labor leaders. His sympathetic attitude toward the working class meant laborers could strike without fear of government suppression. This led to a blossoming of labor unrest. In 1934, 202 strikes broke out across the country. This increased to 642 strikes in 1935, and 674 in 1936. More than 114,000 workers participated. When business groups questioned Cárdenas's tolerance of strikes, he replied that unless it was absolutely clear that industry was right, government would side with the workers.

In the spring of 1936 a new labor organization was established, called the *Confederación de Trabajadores de Mexico*, or the Confederation of Mexican Workers, also known as the CTM. The union's new secretary-general was Vicente Lombardo Toledano, an avowed communist. Unlike CROM, this union was organized on the basis of industry rather than trade, and tried to include the majority of workers. But CTM was similar to CROM in that the government ultimately controlled its function. Cárdenas, in a move designed to prevent Toledano from having too much power, refused to allow peasant groups to join CTM. In the long run, CTM was in competition both with CROM and with industrial unions that declared autonomy from both government unions. So CTM did not achieve its goal of representing everybody.

Cárdenas also believed that Mexico needed a new official national party, one that recognized groups of people overlooked by the PNR. In 1938, he organized one last political convention for the PNR in which members officially established the party's successor, the *Partido de la Revolución Mexicana*, or the PRM. Mexico operates within a single-party system, but Cárdenas's plan was to initiate a party supported by four specific factions: labor and the CTM, agriculture and *ejidatarios*, the military, and civil servants, which included much of the general public. Each sector assigned representatives to public office, thus becoming part of the president's cabinet. Again, the PRM's goal was to represent the majority of Mexicans.

Nationalization of Mexican Oil

Unrest that began in the halls of labor led to one of the most startling acts of Cárdenas's presidency, the nationalization of the oil fields. Under Porfirio Díaz, most of the national oil reserves had been sold off to foreign companies. Despite the declaration of Article 27 of the constitution, which held that all subsoil resources belonged to the nation as a whole, none of Mexico's presidents had been able to face down the formidable foreign interests which demanded that their ownership of the oil fields be respected.

So, in 1936, this natural resource was still being pumped out of Mexican soil for the profit of foreign nationals. To add insult to injury, the foreign oil companies often sold Mexican oil back to Mexicans at a higher price than they sold it in their own countries, and refused to allow Mexican workers in the oil industry to advance beyond low-level management.

This was the situation in 1937, when a sudden rise in the cost of living in the oil-producing areas led the workers to strike for higher wages. The oil workers' demands would have raised company costs by 133 percent; the companies refused to cooperate. Cárdenas ordered a study to determine whether the oil companies could in fact afford pay raises. The resulting two-thousand-page report not only recommended wage and benefit increases, but demanded that Mexicans be allowed to take leadership positions in the industry.

The oil companies agreed to increase wages, but refused to comply with the other demands. By 1938, heated negotiations between government officials and industry leaders reached a standstill. The industry appealed to the Supreme Court, which, on March 1, 1938, decided that the companies should grant a 26-million-peso raise, as recommended by the government study.

When the oil companies refused to obey the order, President Cárdenas decided it was time to address the nation. On March 18, all radio stations suspended regular programming for the presidential address. Cárdenas surprised the nation that night by settling the dispute once and for all. He cited Article 123 of the constitution, and expropriated the oil companies' holdings, saying that allowing them to ignore Mexican laws was equal to giving

Trading Jewelry for Petroleum

President Cárdenas's nationalization of the oil industry gained widespread, in fact almost universal, approval and outpourings of support, as this scene from Pike's Latin American History *demonstrates.*

"Led by Señora Amalia Solórzano de Cárdenas, the President's young and handsome wife, old and young, well-to-do and poor—mainly the latter—as at a religious festival gathered to make, what was to many, an unheard-of sacrifice. They took off wedding rings, bracelets, earrings, and put them, as it seemed to them, on a national altar. All day long, until the receptacles were full and running over, these Mexican women gave and gave. When night came crowds still waited to deposit their offerings, which comprised everything from gold and silver to animals and corn.

What was the value in money of the outpouring of possessions to meet the goal of millions of pesos? Pitiably small—not more than 100,000 pesos—little to pay millions—but the outpouring of women, stripping themselves of what was dear to them, was the result of a great fervor of patriotism the like of which I had never seen or dreamed. It was of little value for the goal. It was inestimable in cementing the spirit of Mexico, where there was a feeling that the Cárdenas move was the symbol of national unity."

up the country's independence. "The sovereignty of the nation," he said, "is thwarted by foreign capitalists who, forgetting that they have formed themselves into Mexican companies, now attempt to elude the mandates and avoid the obligations placed upon them by the authorities of this country."[90]

Cárdenas explained that the country was not confiscating the assets, which would be paid for within ten years. He asked the Mexican people for their support, which they gave in one of the most heartfelt and unanimous outpourings since the early days of the revolution. On March 22, college students, usually critical of the president, rallied outside the National Palace in a show of support. The next day, nearly a quarter of a million people arrived with the same intention. Wealthy ex-revolutionaries donated money to support the government; peasants donated live chickens. Even the Catholic Church endorsed the president's decision. After years of violent struggle, Mexico at last found a government it could believe in.

Foreign governments who had lost the battle were less enthusiastic. Great Britain organized a boycott of Mexican goods. Dispossessed companies tried to prevent the Mexican government from selling its oil on the international market. And although Franklin D. Roosevelt's administration made no overt threats to the Cárdenas administration, the U.S. Treasury stopped purchasing Mexican silver.

The oil fields were turned over to a new government corporation, *Petróleos Mexicanos,* or Pemex. At first, without the high-level management provided by foreigners, the industry suffered a recession. But oil continued to flow, and workers eventually got their raises. Most importantly, Mexico had reclaimed not only one of its most valuable natural resources, but its national pride as well.

The End of the Revolution

Cárdenas's liberal policies began to stir controversy toward the end of his term. In 1938, several of his key cabinet members resigned in order to run for the presidency, and campaigned for a more conservative government. The PRM entered a period of internal crisis as Cárdenas sustained attacks against his socialist regime. On July 7, 1940, Gen. Manuel Ávila Camacho won the presidential election. Cárdenas returned to his home state of Michoacán, and withdrew from the political spotlight completely. He told reporters, "I am no longer the governer, but the governed,"[91] and used his time and money to build a training facility for teachers.

But Cárdenas is still remembered as a successful leader. He rescued Mexico from the corruption of revolutionary caudillos and focused his efforts on rebuilding the country. By the end of his administration, the very word *revolution* meant something much larger than civil war, and people used the term as though it represented a set of ideals fundamental to Mexican identity. Historian Lesley Byrd Simpson writes, "The [National] Party had become the Revolution, and, as its spokesmen said quite openly, if not altogether accurately: 'The Revolution *is* Mexico.'"[92] Even today, the spirit of revolutionary struggle can be detected rumbling beneath the surface of daily life. For this reason, some argue that the revolution has never truly ended.

Belonging to a Nation

Historians place the end of the Mexican Revolution at the end of Lázaro Cárdenas's presidency in 1940, yet the question persists: Is the Mexican Revolution over? When Francisco Madero campaigned for president in 1910, he believed that free elections and freedom of expression were the keys to a new democracy. Emiliano Zapata and his followers clamored for an equitable distribution of land to end the poverty which dehumanized the rural peasants. Still others fought to end the *científico* era of racism and class hierarchies. Did the turbulent years between 1910 and 1940 provide a new social structure capable of solving these problems?

Domination by the PRI

Foreigners looking at Mexican politics soon notice its one-party system. The current party is called the *Partido Revolucionario Institucional* (PRI), and though its name has changed over the years, it has governed Mexico since 1928. Every elected president since that time has been a candidate of the PRI; opposition to it has been largely silenced. And while Mexico may hold free elections, the government is not above manipulating the

results; in 1988, Cuauhtemoc Cárdenas, son of former president Lázaro Cárdenas, claimed fraud when he ran for president as an opposition candidate. Foreign observers agreed that "the PRI has a long history of effective tampering with elections."[93] Three years later, when Cárdenas's party won again in state elections in Chiapas, President Carlos Salinas "jailed 153 Cárdenas supporters in two towns and awarded the victory to the PRI."[94] These can hardly be interpreted as the actions of a traditionally democratic government.

But it would be a mistake to judge the Mexican system by foreign standards. In 1936, President Cárdenas brought together the four strongest interest groups in Mexico: workers, *ejidos*, the military, and the middle class. He called his group the PRM, the Party of the Mexican Revolution. It was supposed to be flexible and ever-changing in order to meet the diversity and evolution of each represented group. Mexican political philosophers claim that this dialogue incorporates all the legitimate interests of the nation, and that one party is sufficient for good, democratic government.

This spirit of cooperative evolution is how the system is supposed to work, and is perhaps what has kept it functioning since 1928. However, the suppression of

Supporters of opposition candidate Cuauhtemoc Cárdenas wave clinched fists in Mexico City, protesting the outcome of the 1988 presidential elections.

dissident voices is an inherent danger of the one-party system. And because the leaders of peasant organizations, labor unions, and other influential groups are all members of the same party, they must beware that the government can undermine their power. As one analyst notes, "If at any time all or part of the *ejido* community supports a political organization other than the PRI, it experiences such unfortunate consequences that, in the end, it will return to the fold."[95] In fact, the PRI accumulated so much power that presidents of the 1980s were thought to

have greater absolute control over politics than their revolutionary predecessors.

Land Reform and Poverty

If Mexico has not achieved the political freedom dreamed of during the revolution, neither has the land reform which the peasants fought for with such zeal been achieved. When the revolution began in 1910, just 260 families owned 80 percent of Mexican territory. To right this situation, under Article 27 of the constitution, the government pursued a policy of land distribution which was active through the 1980s. This has not, however, eliminated rural poverty. Seventy percent of the nation's 40 million poor still struggle to make a living in the sprawling countryside.

Although almost one-quarter of Mexico's population works in agriculture, they receive only 8 percent of the national income. Agriculture accounts for just 7 percent of the country's gross national product, and food still has to be imported to feed the nation's people. Because of this dismal economic performance, President Carlos Salinas de Gortari spent the years of his presidency, 1988 through 1994, reversing some of the major reforms of the revolution. Historians Héctor Aguilar Camín and Lorenzo Meyer explain what the Salinas government did:

> It was necessary to deregulate the economy and the market: to attract foreign investment; to place private investment at center stage; to cross the borders in search of markets, partners, investments, and technology; and to exchange the labyrinth of solitude for the supermarket of world integration.[96]

Finally, he eliminated the constitutional right to government-granted land, reestablished rights of private ownership, and reformed the *ejido* system so that those lands could be sold, rented, or borrowed against.

The Cult of the Presidency

Political analysts Héctor Aguilar Camín and Lorenzo Meyer, in their book In the Shadow of the Mexican Revolution, *describe the role of the presidency in Mexican politics.*

"A president ending his tenure is almost a nobody; an incoming president is nearly everything. As an effect of that institutionalization, the holders of those positions pass from the 'nothingness' to power, and from power once again to 'nothingness.' This is one of the reasons for the stability of the country and one of the characteristics of the presidential institution. It is a position, furthermore, that has immense power in a bureaucratic and patrimonial culture such as Mexico's. In 1970, a president of the republic could distribute among his followers six thousand positions, among the best paid and best regarded of the country; in 1982, the distribution reached ten thousand positions. We are talking of an enormous power to reward, punish, and distribute income, concentrated in a single institution, the most important in the Mexican political system."

Striving to create a market economy in Mexico, President Carlos Salinas reversed many of the reforms made during the revolution. He welcomed foreign investment, reformed the ejido *system, and allowed for the private ownership of industries.*

Industrial Workers and Reforms

President Salinas also devoted a large part of his term in office to undoing the nationalization of industries that had occurred under previous regimes. More than 390 state-owned companies were turned over to private ownership during his term. These included the banks, the telephone company, and, of course, agriculture. Foreign investment soared during that same time. Tariffs dropped dramatically, and by signing the North American Free Trade Agreement (NAFTA) in 1994, Mexico opened her borders wide to the same foreign powers who exploited her resources before the revolution.

Industrial workers have not fared well under recent governments, despite Salinas's efforts to bring a market economy to Mexico. Inflation, which ruled the early 1980s, returned with a vengeance during 1995, diminishing hard-won gains in income. Real wages for industrial and manufacturing workers declined by 31 percent between 1982 and 1988. Unemployment is also rampant, with as many as 25 to 30 percent of Mexico's people out of work at any given time.

Racism and Class Barriers

Despite gains made during the revolution, there are still tremendous class and racial barriers in place throughout Mexico. While the Indian population sees its heritage celebrated in popular art, they are still left out of Mexico's economic advancements. The uprising of the Zapatista National Liberation Army in January 1994 is a symptom of the growing estrangement between the government and the people. The Zapatista army is made up largely of Indian people, who claim they are fighting for both their land and their culture, in the tradition of Emiliano Zapata.

In addition, wealth in Mexico is still concentrated in a very few hands. Salinas's administration made this situation worse; by the end of his term there were twenty-four new Mexican billionaires, while 14 to 18 million people continued

The Re-creation of Mexico

The philosopher and Nobel Prize–winning poet and essayist Octavio Paz describes the effects of the Mexican Revolution in his classic text The Labyrinth of Solitude.

"The revolutionary movement, as a search for—and momentary finding of—our own selves, transformed Mexico and made her 'other.' To be oneself is always to become that other person who is one's real self, that hidden promise or possibility. In one sense, then, the Revolution has recreated the nation; in another sense, of equal importance, it has extended nationality to races and classes which neither colonialism nor the nineteenth century were able to incorporate into our national life. But despite its extraordinary fecundity, it was incapable of creating a vital order that would be at once a world view and the basis of a really just and free society."

A supporter of the rebel Zapatista National Liberation Army stands in front of a mural of Emiliano Zapata. Members of the movement fight in the tradition of Zapata, hoping to maintain the land and the culture of the Indian people.

to live in extreme poverty. It is true that Mexico's middle class has grown since the industrialization of the 1940 and 1950s. And this sector of society is beginning to dominate education, consumer markets, the mass media, and local bureaucracies. Even so, the private sector of the economy remains dominated by a minority of wealthy families.

Political corruption, poverty, and social unrest characterize Mexico today in much the same way they did in the days of Porfirio Díaz. Much of the stability achieved by the Mexican Revolution is thought to have vanished. But as one historian points out, "The revolution, if it did nothing else, produced a nation of people with a national sense, a nation whose art, architecture, and every mode of thought are distinct."[97] If anything has changed, it is the people's sense of belonging to a nation that is uniquely theirs, by right of blood, sweat, and dreams.

Notes

Introduction: After Years of Oppression

1. Francisco Madero, "Plan of San Luis Potosí," in Gene Z. Hanrahan, ed., *Documents on the Mexican Revolution*, vol. 1. Salisbury, NC: Documentary Publications, 1976–1982, p. 62.

2. Frederick Katz, "Mexico: Restored Republic and Porfiriato, 1867–1910," in Leslie Bethell, ed., *The Cambridge History of Latin America*, vol. 5. Cambridge: Cambridge University Press, 1986, p. 77.

3. Alan Knight, *The Mexican Revolution*, vol. 1. Cambridge: Cambridge University Press, 1986, p. 25.

Chapter 1: The Rise and Fall of the Porfiriato

4. John Mason Hart, *Revolutionary Mexico: The Coming and Process of the Mexican Revolution.* Berkeley: University of California Press, 1987, p. 131.

5. Katz, "Mexico: Restored Republic and Porfiriato, 1867–1910," p. 27.

6. Katz, "Mexico: Restored Republic and Porfiriato, 1867–1910," p. 27.

7. Hart, *Revolutionary Mexico*, p. 134.

8. Hart, *Revolutionary Mexico*, p. 142.

9. Lesley Byrd Simpson, *Many Mexicos.* Berkeley: University of California Press, 1971, p. 293.

10. Quoted in Shirlene Ann Soto, *The Mexican Woman: A Study of Her Participation in the Revolution, 1910–1940.* Palo Alto, CA: R & E Research Associates, 1979, p. 4.

11. Soto, *The Mexican Woman*, p. 4.

12. Katz, "Mexico: Restored Republic and Porfiriato, 1867–1910," p. 54.

13. Quoted in Frederick B. Pike, ed., *Latin American History: Select Problems.* New York: Harcourt, Brace and World, 1969, p. 308.

Chapter 2: Leaders of the Revolution

14. Stanley R. Ross, *Francisco I. Madero: Apostle of Mexican Democracy.* New York: AMS Press, 1955, pp. 12–13.

15. Quoted in Ross, *Francisco I. Madero*, p. 46.

16. Knight, *The Mexican Revolution*, vol. 1, p. 74.

17. Knight, *The Mexican Revolution*, vol. 1, p. 57.

18. Quoted in Ross, *Francisco I. Madero*, p. 114.

19. Quoted in Ross, *Francisco I. Madero*, p. 127.

20. William Weber Johnson, *Heroic Mexico.* San Diego: Harcourt Brace, 1984, p. 50.

21. Knight, *The Mexican Revolution*, vol. 1, p. 176.

22. Quoted in Shirlene Ann Soto, *Emergence of the Modern Mexican Woman: Her Participation in Revolution and Struggle for Equality, 1910–1940.* Denver, CO: Arden Press, 1990, p. 34.

23. Henry Bamford Parkes, *A History of Mexico*, 3rd ed. Boston: Houghton Mifflin, 1969, p. 318.

24. Parkes, *A History of Mexico*, p. 319.

25. Ross, *Francisco I. Madero*, p. 154.

26. Ross, *Francisco I. Madero*, p. 166.

27. Parkes, *A History of Mexico*, p. 321.

28. Ross, *Francisco I. Madero*, p. 117.

29. John Womack Jr., *Zapata and the Mexican Revolution.* New York: Knopf, 1971, p. 118.

Chapter 3: Failed Campaign Promises

30. Johnson, *Heroic Mexico*, p. 37.

31. Quoted in Womack, *Zapata and the Mexican Revolution*, p. 127.

32. Knight, *The Mexican Revolution*, vol. 1, p. 311.

33. Quoted in Womack, *Zapata and the Mexican Revolution*, p. 216.

34. Ramón Eduardo Ruíz, *The Great Rebellion: Mexico, 1905–1924*. New York: W. W. Norton, 1980, p. 242.

35. Ruíz, *The Great Rebellion*, p. 135.

36. Charles C. Cumberland, *Mexican Revolution: Genesis Under Madero*. Austin: University of Texas Press, 1952, p. 196.

37. Cumberland, *Mexican Revolution*, p. 201.

38. Ross, *Francisco I. Madero*, p. 232.

Chapter 4: Huerta's Reign of Terror

39. Johnson, *Heroic Mexico*, p. 101.

40. Quoted in Knight, *The Mexican Revolution*, vol. 1, p. 486.

41. Quoted in Ross, *Francisco I. Madero*, p. 307.

42. Quoted in Cumberland, *Mexican Revolution*, p. 237.

43. Parkes, *A History of Mexico*, p. 338.

44. Quoted in Peter Calvert, *The Mexican Revolution, 1910–1914*. Cambridge: Cambridge University Press, 1968, p. 186.

Chapter 5: Chaos for President

45. Parkes, *A History of Mexico*, p. 349.

46. Parkes, *A History of Mexico*, pp. 350–51

47. Parkes, *A History of Mexico*, p. 350

48. Womack, *Zapata and the Mexican Revolution*, p. 296.

49. Quoted in Bethell, *The Cambridge History of Latin America*, vol. 5, p. 119.

Chapter 6: A New Constitution

50. Quoted in Ruíz, *The Great Rebellion*, p. 164.

51. Quoted in Ruíz, *The Great Rebellion*, p. 164.

52. Hart, *Revolutionary Mexico*, p. 331.

53. Parkes, *A History of Mexico*, p. 362.

54. Soto, *Emergence of the Modern Mexican Woman*, pp. 57–58.

55. Johnson, *Heroic Mexico*, p. 322.

56. Quoted in Johnson, *Heroic Mexico*, p. 327.

57. Parkes, *A History of Mexico*, p. 363.

58. Quoted in Ruíz, *The Great Rebellion*, p. 161.

59. Quoted in Ruíz, *The Great Rebellion*, p. 166.

60. Quoted in Womack, *Zapata and the Mexican Revolution*, p. 321.

61. Quoted in Womack, *Zapata and the Mexican Revolution*, p. 322.

Chapter 7: Betrayal and Murder

62. Douglas W. Richmond, *Venustiano Carranza's Nationalist Struggle, 1893–1920*. Lincoln: University of Nebraska Press, 1983, p. 220.

63. Parkes, *A History of Mexico*, p. 359.

64. Richmond, *Venustiano Carranza's Nationalist Struggle*, p. 221.

65. Quoted in Linda B. Hall, *Álvaro Obregón: Power and Revolution in Mexico, 1911–1920*. College Station: Texas A&M University Press, 1981, p. 205.

66. Quoted in Hall, *Álvaro Obregón*, p. 212.

67. Johnson, *Heroic Mexico*, p. 344.

68. Hall, *Álvaro Obregón*, p. 228.

69. Quoted in Hall, *Álvaro Obregón*, p. 230.

70. Johnson, *Heroic Mexico*, p. 350.

71. Johnson, *Heroic Mexico*, p. 351.

Chapter 8: The Violence Subsides

72. Frank R. Brandenburg, *The Making of Modern Mexico*. Englewood Cliffs, NJ: Prentice-Hall, 1964, p. 58.
73. Quoted in Héctor Aguilar Camín and Lorenzo Meyer, *In the Shadow of the Mexican Revolution*. Translated by Luis Alberto Fierro. Austin: University of Texas Press, 1993, p. 114.
74. Parkes, *A History of Mexico*, p. 377.
75. Johnson, *Heroic Mexico*, p. 368.
76. Brandenburg, *The Making of Modern Mexico*, p. 70.
77. Johnson, *Heroic Mexico*, p. 379.
78. Quoted in Johnson, *Heroic Mexico*, p. 372.

Chapter 9: Reform or Oppression?

79. James A. Magner, *Men of Mexico*. Milwaukee: Bruce, 1943, p. 522
80. Magner, *Men of Mexico*, p. 523.
81. Johnson, *Heroic Mexico*, p. 386.
82. Quoted in Johnson, *Heroic Mexico*, p. 392.
83. Quoted in Magner, *Men of Mexico*, p. 534.
84. Soto, *The Mexican Woman*, p. 83.
85. Soto, *Emergence of the Modern Mexican Woman*, p. 117.
86. Quoted in Magner, *Men of Mexico*, p. 551.

Chapter 10: Cautious Progress

87. Quoted in Magner, *Men of Mexico*, p. 555.
88. Quoted in Magner, *Men of Mexico*, p. 571.
89. Brandenburg, *The Making of Modern Mexico*, pp. 85–86.
90. Quoted in Johnson, *Heroic Mexico*, p. 419.
91. Quoted in Johnson, *Heroic Mexico*, p. 422.
92. Simpson, *Many Mexicos*, p. 329.

Epilogue: Belonging to a Nation

93. Christopher Wood, "Mexico: Survey," *The Economist*, February 13, 1993, p. 11.
94. "Mexico: The Revolution Continues," *The Economist*, January 22, 1994, p. 21.
95. Quoted in Stanley R. Ross, ed., *Is the Mexican Revolution Dead?* Philadelphia: Temple University Press, 1975, p. 278.
96. Camín and Meyer, *In the Shadow of the Mexican Revolution*, p. 248.
97. Charles C. Cumberland, *Mexico: The Struggle for Modernity*. London: Oxford University Press, 1968, p. 275.

For Further Reading

Jerome R. Adams, *Liberators and Patriots of Latin America: Biographies of 23 Leaders.* Jefferson, NC: McFarland, 1991. The author includes biographies of Pancho Villa, Emiliano Zapata, and three women of the revolution, Dolores Jiménez y Muro, Juana Belén Gutiérrez de Mendoza, and Hermila Galindo de Topete.

Frank R. Brandenburg, *The Making of Modern Mexico.* Englewood Cliffs, NJ: Prentice-Hall, 1964. A dry but well-documented account of Mexico from the beginning of the revolution through the middle of the twentieth century.

Charles C. Cumberland, *Mexican Revolution: Genesis Under Madero.* Austin: University of Texas Press, 1952. A Texas historian details the early days of the revolution.

David Elliott, ed., *¡Tierra y Libertad! Photographs of Mexico 1900–1935.* Oxford: Museum of Modern Art, 1985. This fascinating collection of photos from the Casasola Archive provides a poignant glimpse at the faces of soldiers, revolutionaries, prostitutes, assassins, and political leaders.

Martin Luis Guzman, ed., *Memoirs of Pancho Villa.* Translated by Virginia H. Taylor. Austin: University of Texas Press, 1965. A bombastic account of Villa's participation in the revolution, as told by Villa himself.

Gene Z. Hanrahan, ed., *Documents on the Mexican Revolution.* 6 vols. Salisbury, NC: Documentary Publications, 1976–1982. This collection contains the exact text of hundreds of documents, both English originals and translations. Series includes: *The Origins of the Revolution in Texas, Arizona, New Mexico, and California, 1910–1911; The Madero Revolution as Reported in the Confidential Dispatches of U.S. Ambassador Henry Lane Wilson and the Embassy in Mexico City, June 1910 to June 1911; The Election of Madero, the Rise of Emiliano Zapata, and the Reyes Plot in Texas; The Murder of Madero and the Role Played by U.S. Ambassador Henry Lane Wilson; Blood Below the Border: American Eye-Witness Accounts of the Mexican Revolution;* and *¡Abajo el Gringo! Anti-American Sentiment During the Mexican Revolution.*

Donald Hodges and Ross Gandy, *Mexico 1910–1982: Reform or Revolution?* London: Zed Press, 1983. This readable, opinionated book includes a summary of revolutionary events in Mexico and a political analysis of how military dictatorships in Latin America have adversely affected their populations.

James A. Magner, *Men of Mexico.* Milwaukee: Bruce, 1943. Though somewhat dated, this book offers worthwhile background on seventeen major male historical figures including Porfirio Díaz, Venustiano Carranza, Plutarco Elías Calles, and Lázaro Cárdenas.

"Mexico: The Revolution Continues," *The Economist,* January 22, pp. 19–21. A look at modern-day economics in Mexico, with special attention on the presidency of Carlos Salinas.

Edith O'Shaughnessy, *Diplomatic Days.* New York: Harper & Brothers, 1917. An eyewitness account by an American woman who lived in Mexico during the early days of the revolution, this memoir is biased but lively.

Henry Bamford Parkes, *A History of Mexico.* 3rd ed. Boston: Houghton Mifflin, 1969. A rich history told in a lively narrative style, filled with information about not only the revolution, but every era since the earliest days of Spanish conquest.

Octavio Paz, *The Labyrinth of Solitude.* New York: Grove Weidenfeld, 1985. Nobel Prize–winning author Paz discusses the history, culture, and philosophy of the Mexican people. He includes a chapter on the Mexican Revolution.

Richard Rodriguez, "Mixed Blood: Columbus's Legacy: A World Made Mestizo," *Harper's Magazine,* November 1991, pp. 47–56. This autobiographical narrative examines the fundamentals of racism against people of Indian ancestry.

Lesley Byrd Simpson, *Many Mexicos.* Berkeley: University of California Press, 1971. This popular book about Mexico includes a chapter about Porfirio Díaz's regime, and two about the revolution.

Shirlene Ann Soto, *The Mexican Woman: A Study of Her Participation in the Revolution, 1910–1940.* Palo Alto, CA: R & E Research Associates, 1979. Information about women of the revolution is hard to find; this is one of the best collections available in English.

Peter Winn, *Americas: The Changing Face of Latin America and the Caribbean.* New York: Pantheon, 1992. Winn was the academic director of the PBS series about Latin America entitled "Americas." This book provides an excellent overview of Latin America's people and history.

John Womack Jr., *Zapata and the Mexican Revolution.* New York: Knopf, 1971. A detailed look at the revolutionary folk hero; provides a perspective on the revolution that is often omitted from more general histories.

Christopher Wood, "Mexico: Survey," *The Economist,* February 13, 1993, pp. 3–22. A comprehensive look at the economic situation in Mexico by a conservative magazine. Lots of facts and figures detailing production and employment.

Works Consulted

Leslie Bethell, ed., *The Cambridge History of Latin America.* 5 vols. Cambridge: Cambridge University Press, 1986. A large collection of essays about Latin America written by a variety of scholars. Volumes 4 and 5 cover events that occurred between 1870 and 1930.

Peter Calvert, *The Mexican Revolution, 1910–1914.* Cambridge: Cambridge University Press, 1968. Calvert discusses the political and economic relationships between Mexico, the United States, and Great Britain during the early years of the revolution.

Héctor Aguilar Camín and Lorenzo Meyer, *In the Shadow of the Mexican Revolution.* Translated by Luis Alberto Fierro. Austin: University of Texas Press, 1993. Two of Mexico's leading intellectuals cover the Mexican Revolution itself, the gradual consolidation of institutions, the Cárdenas regime, and the recent transition toward a new historical period.

Charles C. Cumberland, *Mexico: The Struggle for Modernity.* London: Oxford University Press, 1968. Follows Mexico's history from the Aztecs to the mid-1960s, with emphasis on social, economic, and cultural trends. Contains a chronology of important events and a good, if slightly dated, bibliography.

Linda B. Hall, *Álvaro Obregón: Power and Revolution in Mexico, 1911–1920.* College Station: Texas A&M University Press, 1981. This biography covers the Mexican soldier-politician's Sonoran background through his ascension to the presidency.

John Mason Hart, *Revolutionary Mexico: The Coming and Process of the Mexican Revolution.* Berkeley: University of California Press, 1987. Half of this book is devoted to Porfirio Díaz's regime and its influence on the revolution. Hart focuses on how differently the revolution affected various economic segments of society.

William Weber Johnson, *Heroic Mexico.* San Diego: Harcourt Brace, 1984. A lively, analytical book, filled with details that bring the history of Mexico to life.

Alan Knight, *The Mexican Revolution.* 2 vols. Cambridge: Cambridge University Press, 1986. Volume 1 of this respected analysis focuses on the causes leading up to the revolution, and the complexities of Madero's regime. Volume 2 discusses the violent years of the revolution through Carranza's regime.

Frederick B. Pike, ed., *Latin American History: Select Problems.* New York: Harcourt, Brace and World, 1969. This overview includes a series of readings about the Mexican Revolution, excerpted and translated from historical documents.

Douglas W. Richmond, *Venustiano Carranza's Nationalist Struggle, 1893–1920.*

Lincoln: University of Nebraska Press, 1983. Describes Carranza's political career in detail, including his rise to power, efforts to implement the 1917 constitution, and his overall impact on national affairs.

Stanley R. Ross, *Francisco I. Madero: Apostle of Mexican Democracy*. New York: AMS Press, 1955. This is a thorough, readable account of Madero's personal and political life; presents a sympathetic but largely unbiased view.

Stanley R. Ross, ed., *Is the Mexican Revolution Dead?* Philadelphia: Temple University Press, 1975. This collection of articles projects the effects of the Mexican Revolution into the modern era.

Ramón Eduardo Ruíz, *The Great Rebellion: Mexico, 1905–1924*. New York: W. W. Norton, 1980. This historical account examines the major figures of the revolution, and concludes that Mexico underwent a cataclysmic rebellion that was yet not a social revolution.

Shirlene Ann Soto, *Emergence of the Modern Mexican Woman: Her Participation in Revolution and Struggle for Equality, 1910–1940*. Denver, CO: Arden Press, 1990. This book updates Soto's 1979 book, adding interesting anecdotes and additional factual information about women's struggle to achieve suffrage in Mexico.

Henry Lane Wilson, *Diplomatic Episodes in Mexico, Belgium, and Chile*. New York: Doubleday, Page, 1927. The ambassador's own biased, self-serving, eyewitness account of the early days of the revolution.

Index

Picture Credits

About the Authors

Mary Pierce Frost studied communications and business economics at the University of California, Santa Barbara, then earned a master's degree in English at Sonoma State University. She currently lives in Northern California and teaches speech and communication studies at Santa Rosa Junior College. In addition to writing about Latin American literature and Mexican history, Frost writes poetry and short fiction. Free hours are spent hiking, gardening, and playing piano.

Susan E. Keegan currently lives in Northern California, where she teaches composition, literature, and creative writing at Sonoma State University and Mendocino College. Her many life experiences include earning a master's degree in English, spending years writing for small newspapers, and enjoying a three-month stay in Mexico. She also enjoys playing softball, singing, and watching her fish, cats, children, and flowers grow.